Origami Handcuff Keys:

The Michigan Review of Prisoner Creative Writing, Volume 8

M | LSA PRISON CREATIVE ARTS PROJECT
UNIVERSITY OF MICHIGAN

VOL. 8 – 2016

ISBN: 978-0-578-17839-4

Cover art, *The Unknown* by Jacob Mann

Printed and published by Dakota Avenue West Publishing, LLC

DAKOTA AVENUE WEST PUBLISHING

Detroit, Michigan

www.dakotavenuewest.com

Contents

Prose

Contributors

Editor's Note

This year's volume is dedicated to my friend Tom Engel (1981-2015), whose story "jim" appeared in last year's issue. RIP. See you again.

    —Phil Christman

Acknowledgments

Thanks to the students and volunteers of the Editorial Committee and to my students in English 221, who voted on these pieces, corresponded with contributors and would-be contributors, and generally did most of the work; to the Michigan Department of Corrections, which allowed that work to take place; to Jacob Mann for our cover art; to Shon Norman of Dakota Avenue West, our printer, who is also responsible for layout; and, finally, to everyone who submitted.

Phil Christman

Poetry

James Adrian
How Would You Feel If?

1. You had to live in your bathroom.
2. You had to walk everywhere you went.
3. You had to cut your power off at midnight.
4. You had to share your clothes with someone else.
5. You had to drink contaminated water.
6. You had to eat what someone else chose & cooked for you.
7. You wasn't allowed to see your nieces & nephews who were under 18.
8. You was told what you can & can't do with your own body.
9. You was not allowed to take a bath, only a shower.
10. You was late to an appointment, you was penalized.
11. You was not allowed to go outside for a week, or maybe a month.
12. You had to get your mail read before you got it.
13. You had to get your pictures approved before you seen them.
14. You was told how much furniture you can have and where to put it.
15. You was forced to move house to house, and city to city unexpectedly.
16. You was told that you couldn't practice your religion.
17. You was only able to go to the store once every two weeks.
18. You was stopped by police & searched regularly.
19. You was paid $1.31 a day, & paid every month.
20. You came home and all your property was moved around & tampered with.
21. You could not trust anyone you knew.

Well, this is my life on a daily basis, so when you think times are hard or you got it bad, try to imagine how we feel and put yourself in our shoes… because this ain't living!!!

#Seewhati'msaying

A dragon's fire couldn't pierce my soul
I'll buckle my knuckles until my heart turns cold
Almost like ice, but nearly close to a frost
With ice water running through my veins, I'll remain a boss
So twinkle your little stars with hope and dreams
I'm mean, like between a rattlesnake and a crack fiend
But like magic, my feelings disappear in thin air
Then again, I smile with the notion that I care
So for all those who wish me well, I hope you sleep at night
While I wrestle with the devil's demons because this ain't life
But maybe if I'm buried face down, you'll finally get it
Or I could hide my smile in a cloud, naw… forget it
My wisdom is priceless with a golden dipped pen
Hieroglyphics on a scroll, so history never ends
Can he really change his past, is the question you'll really ask
As you drop to your knees & believe what I just said
Oh sweet memories will become like ashes in the wind
And every friend will begin to pour out liquor at my end
Listen, understanding my pain will grace the front page
Going viral, my rage will hunt you for days
Not like a ghost, but karma tweeted through the earth
Cause atoms to burst, when I cursed this wicked universe
But all through this verse, you was thinking what's worse
To live with this hurt or be carried in a hearse
Now do you understand, some things never can be fixed
I don't know if I'm walking on two or really down six

So now do you know what I'm saying

Grandma's House

I often close my eyes on those cool summer days and
Remember when I didn't have a care in the world
I'd run into my grandma's house and feel a certain degree of
    comfort
I'd see the warm cozy couch, the picture of Jesus and the many
    candles,
I'd see the small statues and old family photos that were took way
    before I was born
And oh yeah! There was a big floor-model TV
And a record player that had a place to play a thing called 8-tracks
Which created music
The carpet was dull and the plants were just there and in the corner
Was my granddaddy's favorite sleeping chair
Which could only be occupied by us when he was not home,
That chair has remained empty for some time now

In the kitchen was a smell that reminded you of a fresh-baked cake
Or sometimes nothing familiar
There was a wood table pushed to the wall with three chairs made
    of cushions,
A refrigerator, a stove, and a small sink
On the table was bread, old newspapers with coupons, and
    occasionally a pie
Or half a cake

The bathroom was small enough that you could sit on the toilet and
    touch the sink
And there was no bathtub
But over the toilet was the picture of the devil
With horns and a long red tail
He was taking a shit, and smoking a cigarette with a tear in his eye
I never forgot that image and I told myself that one day that picture
    will be mine
Why?
I can't even tell you, but it makes sense
But, the most important thing that I always found in my grandma's
    house

Despite all the images that I remember was unconditional love

But now she brings it to me when she comes to visit me in prison...

George Benton
Words Written on a Tree

Scissors cut paper grass
notebooks write things to relieve
emotions ground, walking words just to express,
branches cry with leaves
Emotional gardens,
warm water won't even drink
dripping upon, falling beneath the hard concrete
Sky distance pavements in the streets

House the same, overnight sleep
old stories, relatives used to please
envision moments about the times,
green thoughts fail beyond garage trees
Backyard winds heavy sometimes chase,
No understanding
Questions asked, "Why me?"
summer heat drawn among,
No Communicating

Generation Roots planted still growing
vacant lots together we grew
rocks worrying about something,
they never went through
Window mirror images lost in between
doors screen, anger shattered behind,
what was seen
weather so extreme for family peace

Mornings pass the days,
how things used to be
changes within when it's not even snowing
Heartache from the painful moments
yesterday's lilies, weekend relief,
Orchard disappointment
loving the feeling, when hugs held tightly
together unity without the present tragedy

Family reunions, faces criticize,
tomorrow years of another possibility
Milestone tables, Cafeteria Love Seats
Mountain high down looking
voice unspoken conversations keep
Church Choir voices, microphones reach
backyard heavy winds sometimes face,
what's happening

Planted Roots from generation to generation,
still growing
leaves cry alone, only branches sees
severe thunderstorms become,
apart from raining
peace with family unified together,
we need to believe
pages turn quite neatly,

It hurts, falling out with family
Sunday dinners that lost its meaning
Where's Grandma's educated speech?
hearts broken, broken hearts,
behind the anger, closed doors scream
images find, words talk not to speak
Readings of someone you love,
Books the same we all read

Charles Brooks
If I . . .

If I...
> Choose the streets, you assure me of my demise
> Attempting to disguise the grand plan for the likes of me
> Maybe it works for others, but I see it clearly

If I...
> Choose education, there's lots of bells and noise
> Though I know it's only plays, I'll play along
> You gotta give a little to get a little, according to the song

If I...
> Choose the law, I commit treason against self
> These laws only accumulate wealth for the currently solvent
> Incarcerating those below them: genocide on poor men

If I...
> Choose change of self, to initiate change on the masses
> The powers that be clash, and attempt to shut me up
> In hopes of continual perpetuation of their mind control

If I...
> Choose to hold court in the streets
> Society becomes pugnacious over the legitimacy of my issues
> Misusing the spotlight for their own spin

If I...
> Choose pure ignorance, then I fail all. Equally
> Not only those who root for me, but those I truly dislike
> Are proved right by my refusal to become aware

If I...
> Choose what is necessary to secure just one more day
> Naysayers may nay, but my family is provided for
> Another night of sleep relieved of their night horrors

If I...

Choose nothing, I've still made an impactful decision
Though open to revision, I'll probably never make adjustments
I'll just continue to be the bane of informed men

If I...
Choose

If I...
Exercise my voice

If I...
Become a beacon for the cause

If I...
Am the revolution that my people yearn for

If I. . .

Demetrius Buckley
Letters from Daddy

This is to the girl who has spring in her eyes
& summer up her sleeves: swing sets
will remind you of a growing life, how
      we sit there, first amazed at the accomplishment
of climbing onto the seat all by ourselves,
so excited, overly frustrated—
but don't dawdle, focus. Begin to kick
your fragile legs forward then backward
until the perception of the playground
is sideways. Hold on tight for your own sake, embrace,
you have your daddy's balance, his capability,
& also his weakness that can keep you away
from the scars that you must endure
to understand the things underfoot.
So don't worry too much about falling
or dusting yourself off, our origin is of the dirt
let it be a souvenir of where you came from,
why you're still fighting.

There was a time
when the coagulant assemblage sent warning.
We (your mother & I) never got the message.
only a last minute spotting, jotted footnotes
from the spiritual abroad
letting us in on a secret about human limitations.
I wondered though, full of cold wind
abrading my face in front of that hospital
why was I so sure
of your feral pouring into this cup a new cocktail?

I don't know any other way
how to tell you this but, I may never
get the chance to leave this place. When you notice
I'm not the one helping you
in the kitchen with your schoolwork
or putting your hair (your mother would go crazy)

in tiny ponytails for school.
Will you still find ways to love me, find
strength to hear me explain a repetitive dream—
a dying where no one sung
any of my favorite songs or spoke without first
clearing their voice into the mic. If it helps, which my love should,
will you reread my words
until the soul echoes. *You were my favorite tune,*
the light of my leaving, the reason for these letters.

Grocery Clipping

Don't be afraid of the color of my skin,
fear is no more than a grocery list
left on the fridge, items needed around a fluctuating home,
things you wouldn't dare ask a neighbor for
or accept under any circumstance.
The hard part, especially when it's crowded,
is standing in the checkout line
unloading the loaves of stress
& sacks of B.S. onto the conveyor belt, & doing,
while the line stretches behind you,
what any ordinary american would be doing
when a cashier is scanning their worth. Imagining.

If I had a chance, I'd ask
to be taken apart every day
& each time put back together differently
with the same purpose.
But before combining subtleness of flesh & memory,
let me lie there in pieces for awhile,
away from myself, away from the sequence—
it's easier that way, better when you're disconnected
from it all.

Did you tell her how much you love her—
after all this time, did she believe you?

Only God knows how to cut a man deep
like the grooves rivers gash
throughout the earth.
Someone tell her
to hurry away from the blue flame. Say
it'll feel like ice cream dripping in her lap,
onto her summer dress, then typed
too early on a grocery clipping.

Robert Lee Allen Caldwell
Orwell's Nightmare

Surrounded by painfully drab walls,
painted and painted again,
with countless layers of colors, meant to be devoid of
    all emotion.

A spectrum of gray and pale institutional blues,
    none bright enough to evoke any feeling but surrender.
Everything in this heartless universe: utilitarian
constructed in some hellish assembly line, manned by soulless
    drones.

Every desk, just like the next.
Every sink, just like the next.
Every bed, just like the next.

Any expression of personality or individuality labeled "contraband"
    or "altered state property,"
immediately removed, to be relegated to some room, in the
    bowels of the institution,
where other creations, of those inmates who have yet to admit
    defeat, go to die.

Repetition
Repetition

Even the "Rorschach" patterns worn through the paint on
    the floor,
from countless hours spent pacing by countless inmates,
    look nearly identical in every cell.
The same paths worn down by the declawed and deranged
    tigers at any 3rd rate zoo.
A neurotic tic developed when absolutely nothing natural remains.

The mind frantically reaching out for a foothold.
Even the most basic of acts such as walking, become essential.
A simulation of freedom.

3 steps turn.
3 steps turn.
Rinse and repeat

The dullest torture lies in the monitory.
The lines between days become nothing more than
    notches on a wall.

The state doing its best to grind us down,
to mold us into a tasteless, formless paste,
    just safe enough for institutional consumption.
I find it more difficult, with each passing day, to
    hold on to some semblance of the man I was
    when I arrived.

How long can a swallowed piece of steak fight off digestion?
Hope systematically destroyed at every turn.

Every ritual,
Every interaction,
Every punishment,
Every reward,

Fiendishly designed by some bureaucratic overlord
to ensure that even the word hope tastes rotten in our mouths.
Zombies, without appetites.

Orwell's "Big Brother" is alive and well
and he grows stronger with each passing day, crawling in America's
    prisons.

Time

She is seductive, with a twist of the familiar,
Quick to let you believe an untruth,
Sleight of hand mastered, she is an illusionist of epic proportions.

Most will get lost in her song.
A sweet melody of misdirection and inevitability,
She will sing you to sleep if you let her.

A relationship beyond choice,
You feel a slave to her direction,
Arrows and entropy build her house.

But look close enough and the foundation crumbles.
Hate her mask but find love in her truth,
Search her details to find her heart.

The pain comes from fear,
Afraid of separation,
Until death do you part.

A relationship misconstrued,
Forever is the desire of an unsure heart.
Be present, be aware.

This moment sits outside time, sit with it & hold her hand.
She makes no promises, dance with her & be drunk from her spirit,
Let her whisper sweet nothings in your ear, for she knows no other
    way.

Undefined

We define things born outside of the grasp of
    language, so they can be forced into boxes.
Victims of our compulsion,
Labeled, organized, categorized. Separated.

Potential cut off at the edges, lest they be put in
    another box,
    a new box,
    appropriately defined but never adequate.

It must make us feel safer to think that we have
    a handle on the wild things.
The things without border and lacking in name.

We delude ourselves for the sake of comfort, occasional
    conversation.
We speak of LIFE, DEATH, LOVE and PAIN frivolously
    as if they are independent.
Losing all meaning in an attempt to ascribe one.

Some things are just not at home between the walls.

Electric Zombies

The bell tolls, the market opens,
Distraction sold, attention bought.
Trivial games and electronic spikes color pixels of lives
     lived by other people.

Deeds done, food enjoyed, love given and received from an
     era forgotten.
Everything shared.
Nothing earned.
Convinced we are gods, using fingertips to summon
     worlds.

Pixelation substituted for cells, wires for veins, glass and
     plastic replace flesh.
And touch, beautiful primal, necessary, touch.
Spanning the spectrum of murderous rage to the physical
     manifestations of love.

Altered,
     touch still exists but only in name,
Malformed, reshaped, from an experience to a command,
From flesh to screen.
It's not that we give our lives away,
We never take them out of the box.

Not used or worn, much less appreciated.
Not stored away in the hopes of rediscovery,
Or use for a latter adventure in which we need them
     pristine,
But forgotten.

Not forsaken or traded, but lost.
Not even memories to remind us of what once was,
The ultimate price of distraction,
Our attention bought by others,
Paid for by us.

J.S. Copeman
Right By Me

A bright yellow morning's haze. . .
This judicial oppression making me momentarily sag,
contained humidity's systemic wilt,
purposeless routinely long hours drag.
I've finally noticed too much Green,
in spring's ambitious plan;
I've suddenly noticed too much fear,
center'd Heart of every man.
Stunning my eyes in verdant sights
of everyday things too blinded to see:
the busy Bugs flying low-level missions,
obeying Nature's order to gather.
The raucous Birds screeching and swooping,
searching for things they'd rather.
Waves of sound come and go,
penetrate the restricted Isle of Silence;
the jets and cars from beyond The Show,
enter the still Vacuums of Violence.
A breeze of relief after all these years,
finally ripples across the Lost;
a wave of new hope reminding me,
that nothing was ever worth this cost.

When the M.D.O.C. Yells "Chow"

Penitentiary rules early in the morning telling me this and that. . .
As I shuffle along this desperate path of stultified men racing to eat.
Being watched in the Strange Circus by squawking radios, jangling
    keys.
Asking for menu options that aren't really choices.
"Two drinks ONLY!" "That means one water—ONLY!" Greeting
    sign on wall.
Take one plastic tray, cup, spoon-like fork; take a plastic seat.
Open spot at a dirty table, wipe it down, keep it moving, next man.
There it is, portioned out carefully, food, not very appealing.
Overcooked, undercooked, burnt, hard, soft, raw, mush—
    adversarial
Looks bland to the critical eyes, add hope.
Tastes bland to the talented tongue, add salt.
Some chew fast like eager dogs; others try to enjoy sad events,
    lingering.
As tablemates come and go in the Prison Machine, next man.
Selling, trading. . . "What have you got? Give me! You owe! Ha ha."
"Time's up, you're done! Get up, out you go. No stealing! Empty
    your pockets!"
One last chew, chug of drink, wipe mouth, turn in plastic tray.
Return to State-issued plastic life, chow's over.

Sudden Soliloquy

Please still the silent voice deep inside my head.
Always so critical of all that I do,
nothing ever seemingly good enough.
Pushing me down like a bully,
when all I really need is a hand up.
What's your problem—self?

Your inadequacies is you really want to know.
You can't draw, cut, dig or walk a straight line.
You suck at everything!
Math, science, history, and geography.
Ugh! You're stupid.
Don't even want to list all of your "problems". . .
as it would take far too long.
See. . . right there, you're impatient as well.
Face it, you're all-fucked-up. AFU.
Why don't you think about killing yourself?
Oh that's right. You have—what happened to that, huh?
Couldn't do it because you're cowardly, too. Great.
Well. . . you did at least try, though, I'll give you that much.
Still. . .
I'm disgusted.

But then I was always reading, discovering magic.
Finding lonely company in the power of books.
Reading about characters by Victor Hugo, Dumas, Voltaire, and
    Sartre.
Don't forget Swift, Kafka or Vonnegut. Especially Kurt!
Bringing you back up when you were down.
So down.

Suddenly making some of those words your own.
Must be fulfilling, or filling the void, eh?
It is, especially if it works.
Oh yeah?
Yes, sometimes people like what I write.
No! I don't believe you.

Yes, they tell me that, too.

Say I'm "honest" and "opening up," to keep going.

You're kidding. You? You lie all the time.

No, I've changed.

But still. . . What is that? Nothing but empty words, right?

Yes and no, it depends on your perspective and intent, I suppose.

But there's POWER in them. I've since learned the truth.

With words you can start a fire. Or a revolution.

Or you can create something spectacular that will last for time
    immemorial.

No way!

Yes, and I've since found that I can erase things, too.

No, you can't!

Sure. . . watch, I'll show you.

Don't. . . please! Come on. . . I need you, I love you!

You don't love me, sorry, but we're done.

Good-bye.

Bye.

Big Yard

A scheduled gathering of random design for state-issued orange
    dots…
Like windblown convicted spores spread across the prison yard,
    drifting
Some mingle in groups among the sea of individuals, difference
Most sharing historical fictions and telling pointless
    autobiographies, deceptions.
Seeking social associations or pleading institutional brotherly bods,
    devotion
To nothing in all honesty but the sentence they must ultimately—
    deserve
There's gregarious Rick greeting his friends as they pass, effusive
And miserable Aaron, the barber of Kincheloe, cutting and
    complaining, egregious
The Apostle Paul preaching the gospel of the weight pit, ecclesiastic
Bipolar Joe's chemically maintained moderate mode, egotist
Long-lost George an exile of the Maple Leaf, he finds himself,
    ejected
finally, persnickety Jack is the walking writer on the wane—
    egressing
"What they got?" Meaning the menu, the high point of the day,
    breakfast
Another allotment of "…with potatoes" for lunch and dinner, banal
"Got a tray for sale! Pizza for sale! Let's trade," business
"Give you two soups or a soap, maybe two desserts," barter
"Hell no! Give me your chicken for my cookie and eggs tonight?"
    bargained
"You've got it my man," to seal the deal they call it a—"Bet."
Report to the desk, the podium, the Control Center, the sergeant
    calls, ticket
A written misconduct for unlimited violations in a petty, theatre
Of the absurd to punish the punished which only creates, tension
That's the only solution they have, it's nothing but bad, theory
As every day is the same, we're all just playing the game, thesis
Because in the end it's really nothing more than simply marking—
    time.

Cognitive Long Dissonance

[dial tone]. . . wuuuuuu...
Beep, boop, beep beep, boopity-bleep... boop.
whirrrrrrr...
Beep. Thank you for calling the Michigan Department of
Corrections Automated Call Center. If you are still living in the
1970s and calling from a rotary dial phone, please stay on the line
and we will notify a time traveler to rescue you from 20th Century
technology. Nah... not really. But hold the line anyway and we will
get back to you at at our earliest convenience. So, at the tone, please
press... 1 to enjoy some Muzak of that era. [tone]...
Boop.
Beep, boop, beep beep, boopity-bleep... boop.
Beep. Thank you for calling the Michigan Department of
Corrections Automated Call Center. If you are calling from
a touch-tone phone and have a burning desire to speak with
an actual, living and functioning being with charm, patience,
understanding, and compassion... well... this number may not
be for you. However, we are bound by the implicit direction and
mutual understanding of a consent decree to keep the lines of
communication open and available to the public. That's unfortunate
but true. So, at the tone, please press... 2 and we will be in
compliance. As you know, we in corrections live to serve.
[tone]
Beep.
We're sorry, your call cannot be completed or answered by an
actual human right now. As the thin blue line is stretched awfully
thin these days. It's definitely Obama's fault! Please try your call
again later when the so-called economic recovery allows necessary
government agencies, such as this one, enough revenue to be able
to hire more people. Maybe then we will be able to spend our
valuable time and resources in the pursuit of answering your most
welcome calls. Which, we assume, must be of the highest quality
and utmost priority to even bother with, huh? Now... you see, the
thing about telecommunications is the volume of dropped... *click.*
[dial tone] ....wuuuuuuu....
Beep, boop, beep beep, boopity-bleep... boop.
Beep. Thank you for calling the Michigan Department of

Corrections Automated Call Center. If you are calling to inquire about our many services provided to and on behalf of a prisoner, please press S for sure-we'll-get-right-on-that. As we in critical government agencies were specifically set up to cater to the various wants and needs of the general public—in regards to their family and friends in prison. Maybe they wouldn't be there now if you had shown this much concern a while ago. Did you ever think of that, huh? Anyway, at the tone, please press... 7. *[tone]*
Beep.
You have selected 7... We're sorry, but there are no services currently available for prisoners at this time. We only warehouse. Please try again when, say, the U.S. Supreme Court overturns such egregious landmark decisions as *Sandin v. Conner* or *Wolfe v. McDonnell.* Thereby restricting their already limited constitutional rights down to the barest fraction of a substantive level—say somewhere about a notch or two above North Korea. That's just about where we want to be. After all, why should criminals have ANY rights? Something we find personally offensive. Until such time... maybe then we'll talk. *Click.*
[dial tone]. . . wuuuuuuu. . .
Beep, boop, beep beep, boopity-bleep... boop.
Beep. Thank you are calling to inquire about *[tone]* transfers; *[tone]* account discrepancies; *[tone]* civil rights violations; *[tone]* or the thousand and one other various demands and complaints we receive... ugh! daily. Then please feel free to press... 0 and answers to life's mysteries will flow. *[tone]*
Beep.
Operator. How may I direct your call?
Click!
[dial tone] wuuuuuuu........
Beep, boop, beep beep, boopity—bleep... booop!
Beep. Thank you for calling the Michigan Department of Corrections Automated Call Center. If you are calling to inquire about employment within an extremely professional organization that treats its employees with the highest degree of courtesy and respect; that offers a competitive benefits package and a living wage that ranks one out of the top five within the tri-state area. One of the best in the country! Not too shabby, eh. Who says that crime doesn't pay? We don't. It pays top scale. So if you are ready

for a rewarding career full of opportunities: paid vacations and sick days; abundant overtime; rapid advancement; educational assistance; compensated stress leave with first-rate psychological counseling available—then boy… do we sure have a spot open for you! Think about it, now is the time to take up the challenge, like joining the Marines. A chance to serve and be stationed in remote locations scattered throughout the state (albeit in underpopulated communities with collapsed industries). At least the housing situation is a buyer's dream! And then you'll be working in an "exciting" environment, surrounded by the friendliest convicts of every… ahem… stripe. Fully supported by the administration and allowed to utilize personal initiative in the ever-elusive definition of the word "authority." After all, we ARE the Michigan Department of Corrections, our motto states: "Expecting Excellence Every Day," pretty much says it all in a nutshell. So what are you waiting for, huh? Oh yeah… at the tone, please press… '6-3-6-2.' (M.D.O.C.) Do it. Do it now!
Click!!!

Grant Czuj
Burning Bullet

-for Brianna

A voice can take us places,
places sometimes familiar and wanted,
pleasant to the nose and eye.
Sifting through the cool dark waters
of our memory—black
starless water like ink. Past
bodies are pulled up from the
rusty sieve, easy and persistent.
Blissful bodies in peace.
Woeful bodies in ruin.
Cheery bodies doubled over in laughter.
We fish to catch ourselves.
The triggers of our memories can
be so so fast and crisp,
sending the emotions of the past
through us like a burning bullet—
a red-hot hunk of drama ripping
through bloody viscera. Just there.
There in front of us again,
everything we've felt, to laugh
about and to kick ourselves over.
The witty immature remarks.
The kindness and the smell
of our hearts' flower blossoming.
Her voice had done that for me.
I had thanked her for it,
and said in a pure truth that
it was good to hear her voice
again.

Skipper

He waves his hands at the sides of
his hairy face when he explains to me
of the zoning out that he does toward
the noise of the yard, the housing unit, the
devilish wholesale controlled chaos of the
prison compound in general. His eyes covered
by cheap dark sunglasses, and his head
covered by a blue and weathered ball cap.
Scruffy black and gray beard and his
shoulders covered by thin layers of dandruff
that fall from his scruff.
He is miserable and he can't understand it.
His New England boyhood—the mental
conservatism—of pretty little houses
and women in their bright floral dresses,
and the colorful flowerbeds, and
everything as cute as a button.
the images of his memories
cannot comprehend the scenes of the red
biohazard bags for the bloodspill cleanups
after a gang fight. Blood and shit and
empty Vaseline tubes in the shower drains;
nobody likes the talk of that. The
faded and old and heavily used
porno mags for rent. Locks clipped to
the ends of belts to fracture
facebone and leave crude openings.
All of the world's laughter is beginning
to seem false and ill-gotten for him.
Who can smile in such a place?
he must ask himself. His face and
hands contort in exaggeration when
the words UNBELIEVABLE and SO
and INCREDIBLE roll out of his
Eastern Sailor's mouth. Just a year
ago in the Caribbean, St. John being
his favorite island. It's UNBELIEVABLE

how he is now here with me, he always
says. No offense to me of course.
It was a large plastic fantastic, he says.
A large fiberglass catamaran, sleek
and new. He was the captain of the vessel.
The owner, a German techie
billionaire. Sunshine and bright blue
waters and sexy women and tropical
storms and cold beer and a private chef
and a decent salary to live it all.
Somehow in Michigan, then a gun,
some physical force, a few well placed
threats, and the wrong senorita to
mess with now keeps his Eastern Sailor
self in shambles and tangles and
confusion. Here with me as I listen to
him and walk with him around and
around the shabby yard through
gangsters and bodybuilders. His daughter
is a lifetime away. But don't mention
that, that's bad form.

Chris Dankovich
The Elevator

I just woke up from a dream I had about you last night
we rode up in an elevator, ever so slow, looking out at the light
from the sun setting on clouds kissed red from its glow,
you as I imagine you to be, and I as I am now.
It's been 8 years, over half as many as we were alive back then
when you were a girl who was a woman, and I a boy who thought
    he was a man,
and I held you in my arms but never made another move
because I knew you to be close I needed nothing to prove to you
but to be something more I might need to be something more
that I could have been then, so we left it there.

Back to the dream: we stood mere inches away
and you lifted me out of the dark in the same way that you always
    would do;
and then the dream did what dreams always seem to do:
I ask if you'd let me buy you coffee, which you did, and we were
    back on the rise
in the lift as the sun set and I looked in your eyes
just like I did with the paper pictures you sent me until I was almost
    19 years old,
that spirit that kept me company on the wall by my bed while you
    wrote me your soul.
Five years have passed since the last picture and 8 since I last heard
    you speak;
you were older, and stronger, but still wore those Summertime
    freckles and mischievous smile
and your voice still echoed like an angel ready to cry.

While in the dream I followed, like a disciple at the last supper,
every word that you said,
I lost the meaning of your words this morning while I was lying in
    bed,
trying to call you back to me with my eyes closed, arms around my
    pillow, but instead
my eyes adjusted to the dark, for the sun hadn't yet risen like it had

in the dream
and I reconstructed, re-lived, something that had never really been,
but which I held on to with all my heart
and we were together again after 8 years apart.
I smiled in the dream and I smiled for real
and I felt the same as I used to feel around you.

You smiled like the waning moon smiles at the stars
and I pulled you into my arms as you held me in yours.
Not even God with a crowbar could pry us from one another
then only our heads parted so we could gaze into each other.
I was nothing but my lips as I kissed yours and I was nothing but
    our kiss.
When I woke I cried and prayed and hoped and wished
to go back 5 minutes and not even 8 years
because 5 minutes ago I loved you and 5 minutes ago you were
    here.
And though I told myself that none of this really happened,
the feeling didn't fade.

Even in a dream we must breathe and so our lips parted,
the air in between us as gentle as when the kiss started.
I looked at you and you looked at me,
and we were all each other could see.
Then the elevator chimed and you walked out the door
I let you fade away just like I did before (in real life).
That's when I woke up, looking around, knowing you're not there,
I closed my eyes to find you, to bring you near again,
because I would give up anything real
to have one more moment with you
to do whatever it is you do
with one moment with someone who saved you.

Apology

-To K, E, H. . . though probably D, S, M, and J deserve it too

What can I say to the person
whose love I've abandoned, betrayed?
It makes no difference that it
happened so quick—
in the fire of the moment
that's destined to last
forever as the echo of death
of a connection that was a pillar of my life.

I never meant it so,
but how far can intentions go
into Hell to retrieve a mutual soul?
And will it look back before it gets out
and be forever trapped—
or become like a wraith, undead,
trying to eat us alive?

"But why?" I imagine
you asking in this imaginary conversation
(pain in your eyes, anger at me—even though
this is merely a fantasy).
And why is the question I've
been asking myself over and over;
as if finding the answer would
convince you somehow to return to my life.

Why? is easier than answering what
I was thinking, or else Freud would
have found himself out of a job.
What if I could go back to when
this occurred and begin anew?
But despite all my prayers,
God won't grant me a second attempt
at seconds or years. . . would you?

This is not an apology, though
it would be that too
if I ever spoke to you again—
but I've no magical spells
to resurrect what's gone,
and I'm afraid if I did
I'd merely open up wounds
of how you were wronged.

Instead I write a eulogy
to what I've lost and may have been.
A speech I must give, even if
you won't forgive
so that at least I won't
sin again.
And to answer the reason why—
in that moment I didn't put you up as high
as you earned your place to be. . .

A mistake I've learned from now
and will not make twice. . .
If we see each other in the afterlife
may it matter there that
I've tried to make things right.
(But is that enough in this life?)

Then I will wait until the fates
will turn back time
and I could make the mistake not once,
and only then will I no longer merely say
if only I. . .
if only I. . .

Skipping Stones

Bury your burdens with me.
I'll take them all in and
you'll never see them again.
Whisper your worries,
your doubts and despairs.
I'll keep them all in, like
I'm not even there.

Prayer. . .
those words muttered into air,
pleading and begging that someone will care.
—I'm here—
though no one else was ever there.
Maybe we both can find a way
to have nothing left to fear.

Cast off your cares into the ocean-wide,
funeral pyres burning off to the side.
Smoke fogging the air, waves crashing a sound,
You could help me up, or I might pull you down.

"And Thus Responded Man"

"Then Moses said to God, "Indeed, when I come to the children of Israel and say to them, 'The God of your fathers has sent me to you,' and they say to me, 'What is His name?' what shall I say to them?" And God said to Moses, "I AM THAT I AM."
-Exodus 3:13-14

I am crazy
I am sane
I am happiness
I am pain
I am safety
I am free
I am danger
I am tyranny
I am a lawman
I am an outlaw
I am guarded
I am raw
I am elite
I am like the rest
I am strength
I am weakness
I am pagan
I am Christian
I am an Atheist
I am human
I am chaos
I am order
I am a civilian
I am a soldier
I am clean
I am a germ
I am God
I am a worm
I am courage
I am dread
I am alive
and I am death.

I am everything there ever was
I am everything there will ever be
I am none of the above.
I am only me.

The Shadow of Death

—You—I don't know your name,
but this accusation needs someone identified
as the accused, so I'll call you
"Guy" (as in Guy Fawkes, Guy Hardy. . .
not just some guy. I'm not generalizing
here).

You are why we can't have anything nice.
You are why "They" generalize.
You are why my best friend will die here.
You are why I will not receive a second chance.

I don't think you ever saw me.
When you tried to rape a lady I like moderately well
across the hallway from me
and she screamed, I ran to the door
see you running away.
It was too late for me to do anything, and
I swallowed my basic instinct of compassion
so that I wouldn't be seen standing over
whatever you did to her.

She turned out alright.
She didn't fall down as easily as I imagine
you anticipated.
Good thing for her.
Lucky for you—they now can't
prove more than a simple assault.
But what they can prove is different
than what we both know.

And I could look into your soul,
the book of shadows of your past,
and see the darkness, shade covering black.
And in the darkness where you were born
(some would say spawned,
after the fact looking back)

soiled pools breed disease.

And a virus works by infecting its host
and replicating itself.
So... who coughed on you?
Who sneezed when you were more than
just a zombie, spewing contagions?
Were they more than one too?

And I listen as you stumble by,
head turned upward towards the sky.
A rotten smell from between your teeth,
life crushed beneath your dragging feet.

Once you were a child, doing childish things.
What convalescence of events
on the spark of your being
ignited such a fire
that desires
to destroy, destroy, destroy?

If I could erase the damage done to you...
but once gone, there would be nothing left.
What could have been a magnificent tree,
cut, leaning perilously,
threatening anyone who walks near.

You were given a chance, taken from me,
and ate it in front of all to see,
cannibalizing our future,
relieving yourself of our past.
You are why this curse will last
a thousand generations, or at least a few
until everyone I know is dead.

"They" say we are all alike, but if there
were any similarities, none are any longer left.
I've gnawed off the infected site and chosen life,
while you emanate and worship death.

Marco de'Lor
Would You Bite the Apple?

Have you ever slid in the abyss of temptation. . .
Unparalleled words and steps in buried translation. . .
Desiring the Vacancy within a hooded Vacation. . .
Needing a pocket restoration. . .
Voyaging in a Liberal and lofty local location. . .
Preying on a healthy and wealthy money mission. . .
Only fishing in night Vision,
Ignoring what you're risking. . .
Not Noticing what's missing. . . Maybe your logic & reasoning. . .
Or the fear of Dear "KARMA" Visiting. . .
Could it be behind a barrel. . . In the grips of a guy who goes by
    Darryl,
Willing to deliver your last loud-light Flash in the past
When you were only Ash,
Possibly the lack of dignity or decency,
Maybe missing the sense found in the—Cortex. . .
Maybe the Cranium. . . Next to a Cerebrum. . .
Behind your Cerebellum. . . wherever it comes From. . .
You simply denied it and chose dumb,
See I Lusted and Learned the hard-way. . . Only left
Leading and Living my Legacy in M.D.O.C's hostile hallways,
Where it's no Fame. . . Literally No game. . .
NO OUNCE of shame to claim-blame for a tragic lost
Frame. . . IN FACT it's all the same. . . Except. . .
NO Future and not one DAME. . .
NOT A whisper of beauty to Ever call your NAME. . .
Just the brutal Rain and you left to gain. . .
Envy and betrayal From a lame,
Or a cell-mate named Cane who every-Night causes you
PAIN. . .
See for me I finally see what it took. . .
Would you still bite the worm if you knew it was on the hook. . . ?
Some clues aren't clear when Viewing life as a Crook. . .
I viewed better views in my Cell out of a book,
Some old and wise Opened my Eyes to a whole new paradigm. . .
ALL gold ain't good & most shine ain't divine. . .

Yet the real-rich wine resides right in your mind. . .
In the roots of the Vine that feeds your climb. . .
Motivating Voices of great choices that always seem to rhyme. . .
Time has proved walking the righteous line. . .
In the long run you'll be fine. . .
It's the Idol-shrine of Crime that causes us to go Blind,
just clear your gaze. . . you'll see your way through
Life's complicated maze. . . Only made as a Phase. . .
To raise character beyond your age. . .
Leading your trail-blaze towards wonderful days,
Because being righteous isn't found in a temple. . .
Upon or behind a pedestal. . .
Nor through a narrow peep-hole. . .
It's all so simple. . . and Possible. . . maybe Inevitable. . .
Just being able and Capable of denying The
APPLE!

Rebecca Fackler
Me vs. H.D.

I'm giving Humpty Dumpty
a run for his money.
Let's see who has more shattered pieces,
you've got nothing on me,
you fragile weak egg.
My pieces? They too have pieces.
The haughty king's horses
just trampled on me,
the grandest of stampedes.
And all the king's men
laughed at me,
and sang, "What a merry fuck was she."
Cry if you want
over your damaged shell.
I'll sob and I'll bleed for my soul.
At the end of it all
remember this well:
> At least they thought *you* were worth fixing.

John C. Gaik IV
The Last Days Club

We were among friends of the Last Days Club saying good
    riddance and leaving paradise together,
I preferred to focus on the dreams ahead;
The big sleep,
Wake me up when spring comes.

I want to emerge from the depths like a seedling from the earth,
I want to awake being held with your motherly eyes upon me;
Nestled deep in the forest clearing's wild flower fields;
Where the bumblebees hum the vacuum chorus.

In my youth I wanted to know the deepest loves,
On the other hand, I wanted to know the dying and the dead,
At least get a taste on a few nights;
I fear I've come far closer to reaching those goals than I had ever
    hoped I would in the end.
Can I take it back?

Wake me up when spring comes.

M.G. Glenn
Dionysian Dream

Walking through this Garden, I gaze upon the truth,
      Hidden in a riddle, but ancient in its youth
Where origami blossoms, bloom on stems of bone
Through broken, bloodied soil where all wickedness is grown.

      The lady of the flowers, covered in tattoos
Blends into the wilds, child's eyes cerulean blue
      Where a spider's web's afloat, tinged a rainbow hue
Woven through the willows with a beast upon a noose,

Guarding Dionysian grapes, grown on Celtic knotted vines
      Crimson plump and bloody, meant for satan's finest wine
My lady hums a tune, and draws a rune to call the feast
      Notes woven in a loom, it seems the tune enchants the beast
The orchard safe to enter, I harvest my affliction
      My baskets fill with grapes, intoxications my intention
Skipping like a child, my fingers scratched and torn
Yet for all my wits and guile still I can't avoid the thorn
      So into my bitter blood I let the poison seep
As I lay beneath the trees and watch the darkness slowly creep.
My horizons bruised and purple the spiders now descending
      From crooked little corners and broken webs amending
My lady she attends me rested head upon her breast
      Swallowed by the willows as the sun it creeps the crest
Earth and vines cocoon me drawn now deep within
      The forest joins the chorus as I feast upon my sin.

Norman Hile
Just a Moment of Understanding

The piercing blast of the horn was incongruous to the peaceful surroundings of the neighborhood. The chirping serenade of the nearby winged orchestra halted. Ferocious felines scampered to their favorite layers of safety. Casual conversations among the weathered picket fences were diverted. The rude interjection into the serenity had disrupted the lives of nature and man. Daniel had the most inopportune fortune to be the intended recipient of the aural assault. He was seated behind the wheel of his stationary vehicle. It was in the path of the man who had just ceremoniously announced his presence directly behind. What could be the rush? This rash impatient action perplexed Daniel's philosophy. Life was to be absorbed, taken with each moment's appreciation. To miss any by haste is an affront to the gift of possessing a sentient soul. Each moment exhibited an intrinsic value exceeding beyond the immediate physical palpitations of the present. Every fiber of nature contributes its lesson in life and Daniel is an inured student, staving off the intruding lassitude that indifference will foster.

But Victor, the guilty assailant of the peace, knows nothing of Daniel's classroom. In his plane of existence there was nothing more than the vacuous movement of banality. Going from one requisite event of the day to the next. The philosophy that all is just a procession of scenes in the theater of the day eroding the finite course of life. Victor, being devoid of any activity outside of his own single-mindedness, fumed at the temerity that his counterpart's hindrance possessed. What could be the holdup? There are appointed places to go and predescribed people to see! These dates with unchangeable destiny must be fulfilled so as to complete the inane doldrums of the inevitable. Just get this day over with. Just get this life over with.

Possessing no further patience, Victor pulled hard on the wheel, stomped on the gas, and lurched the vehicle ahead toward his predestination. But shortly the screech of braking tires was heard. Coming up short, after so little progress, Victor's vision beheld the purpose of Daniel's recalcitrance. Directly in front of Daniel's car was a small boy. The boy's knees and elbows were scraped and bloody. Tears of fright were streaking down his cherubic face. The white and saline paths evident among the soil clouding his cheeks. The boy's legs were tangled, intertwined within his twisted bicycle. The front wheel still spinning with the tica-tica-tica of the attached baseball card reverberating its rhythm against the spokes.

Daniel, surprised by the screech of the tires, craned his neck to capture the scene. His eyes brought clarity to his mind as to what the immediacy of his offender had been. In the front seat, next to Victor, was a woman. She was breathing heavily, sweat pulled up on her brow and face. There was distress in her countenance and the enlarged abdomen testified to the veracity of the labor of birth by which she was encumbered.

Daniel gaze rose to meet the leer of Victor. As the assumed antagonist and protagonist's eyes met therewith was found a lucid moment of shared reality that connected them in the fraternity of humanity. A fraternity that often is devoid of communal participation, responsibility, or respect. If each person could only practice empathy and tolerance our world could be what for an instant both Daniel and Victor realized. They had shared. . . JUST A MOMENT OF UNDERSTANDING. . .

Gabriel Jagniecki
Ode to Luney

Eyes like Jimi
Glazed and droopy
  search This World for meaning!
pickin' and ah sinin'
His fingertips they blaze
cauterize
His heart that's bleeding
my Heart that's fiending!
He's a lot older now. . .
you would've thought
he done learned a little
on these infested prison yards
  But He's Back Baby!
Comin ta getcha'!
Well, he ah
Little bit lost on
The role of "function"
But he sure can play that
"guit-fiddle" that "six-string" that "AXE"
He'll make these fences bend
AND the C.O.'s dance!
Eyes like Jimi
Seeing screamin' fans again!
We ain't in prison no more sir!
On this decrepit pic-nic table
amidst the hissing yard
He's seeing stars!
While he's pluckin' them strings
Just one more little ditty
  As his stained skin sags
One more gaping toothless grin
To show you
What freedom really looks like!
Eyes like Jimi
Those fingertips
Are dancing flames

gropin' that slick wooden neck
feeling out a reason
He took a break, scratched his face
those glazed eyes looked up at me
as he said,
"gabe it's all about repetition"
"wax on wax off"
"The Spiritual Journey does not come easy"
I had to laugh
And you know
I had to listen

Darnell L. Jett
A Loving Child

Suffocating while she's debating the particulars of my fate
Reality beckons
As sand slips through the hourglass of God's fingertips
Sending me forth from these full hips
Parental intuition outgrew all future ambition she once had
Introducing me to a world
Filled with the things she was never blessed with
GOD
Only if she knew I knew
That I'm getting heavy and her arms tired
Well at least that much
Cause when her eyes say such
I just feel crushed knowing I depend on her so much
And the audacity of this Hades baby a 80s Baby
For calling me a Maybe's Baby
Just to take care this ugly lady's baby like I'm not cuter than cute
Ma, I glad you gave this the boot
See you're the real soldier salute
So I might just stomp this dude when I learn to walk
Or even curse this man out when I learn to talk
Cause not that I'm outside of you
Nothing matters outside of you
And to that I remain true
And for everything you missed in life I promise to catch
And to make mentioning you before honoring any of my success
As fulfilling as drinking the milk from your breast
Sincerely a loving child

Back When

Maybe as the hours fade and now gives way to a now not yet
    formed maybe we could conform
You Know
Into something
Somewhere warm
Un-torn
Light-years away from the scorned
Yet, honestly
I promise
I can't recall ever having been so honest
Especially when I still would, Piss on Patience and rush to the pain
    that paints your lips
So maybe
And I mean MAYBE
So as the two ship that pass in the dead of night under low light
    fearful of the danger of just
        a TOUCH
That analogy best fits US
Yet
Unlike them I see you
Yeah, I see You
Your eyes always seems to find some glimmer of the moon
Though which I view this growing typhoon waiting behind me
And as I pray to the one who designed me, for an inkling of the
    mercy absent in your gaze
And the words of this poem solidifies between the margins of a
    page
Nothing Changes
Yet instill
I still recall when you would call
And I could, call you my queen
Back when the ends somehow seemed, to justify the means
See, what I mean is ahhh. . .
DAMN YOU MEAN
Like, what you mean this don't feel right
When everything you left is RIGHT HERE
RIGHT NOW

Writing this poem
In hopes of getting you RIGHT BACK
While I'm staring RIGHT UP at this wave
And Yo' Ass Know I can't swim
I mean
Even when things seemed dim
Back when it was just Us-Vs-Them
I was like fuck them
 Cause regardless how we would fight
And you did things I didn't like
At the end of the night
You represented my light
You know
Back when situating our situation just took a mere conversation
And we wasn't left contemplating about who's wrong and what's
    right
But like I said
Maybe as the hours fade
And now gives way to a now not yet formed
Maybe we could conform
You know
Into something
Somewhere warm
Un-torn
Light-years away from the scorned
I just pray I don't drown in the process

Asia Dominique Johnson
Rosedale Park

Disney and dolls miles
away from the taste
lust first kisses unlocked
chastity Green Ingenue
wide eyes looking
searching plus and pineapples
fruits not forbidden innocence

that of a 6-year-old girl

Springtime in Eden 1992
they foolishly let him in
let sin in to
extinguish her light ignite
the flight of white doves

from her Princess Jasmine panties

Ponytails in penguin pajamas
pajamas he sent for her
when all was silent
in the world vibrant
in Shirley Temple curls

He stiffened

Should have played
opossum not some
reckless hunt through
a delicate snare
assembled kindled

what should have been

Mouth watered despite her
being someone's daughter

slaughter her like a lamb damn

illicit chimera

> No force wasn't gagged
> and bound no sound escaped
> when he took to her
> unripe lips eclipsed
> by his 30-year-old
> flame as vanilla ice cream
> dripped down her
>
> diminutive hand

Patrick Kinney
We Are

Zero-point particles
or indefinitely twisted
chords aquiver
singing the life electric

mostly empty space
like packing peanuts or cosmic cotton candy
wave-form potentialities
more wondrous and unfathomable
than a million angels
dancing on a pinhead

obeying laws involuntarily
writ before the eyes of God
opened from the mind
of homo australopithecus

built one and one together
negative attracting positive
reacting, contracting
self-aligned in periodic stages
columns characteristic
of condensed energy from collapsed stars

step-wise and stage-dependent
ever since the singularity was
and we were one

and still are
zero-point particles
random chords aquiver
dancing through
this life electric

Slammed Gently

Iron plates
slam in sand
muscles stretch
and I stand

stronger
as the breeze blows past
the breeze on shirt on skin on knees

drying sweat, feeling free
snatching iron

gently

Cannot Be Released

Quiet, respectful
cleanly and neat
keeps to himself
but cannot be released

for something he did
long, long ago
before his voice deepened
before he had grown

he regrets it a lot
we don't doubt that he does
everyday he works hard
to reform who he was

but we just can't get over
the offense he committed
twenty years, thirty years
how much time enough is it

what is life, what is death
when is punishment ended

what makes forty years better
than a straight up death sentence

will it change what he's done
will it make us feel better
will it stop other kids
or just make him a debtor

from one institution
to another he'll go
from a hard life in prison
to a soft old-folk's home

That's if he survives
life expectancy's lower
could get stabbed in the shower
or stomped to death on the floor

But when all's said and done
we just keep coming back
to the crime he committed
you can't blame us for that
for his victim had not
one more second of life
nor his family to know
what it might have been like

Second chances are nice
were it us, we'd say give it
but it's not our lives
and it's not our kid, is it?

So no matter how quiet
or respectful and neat
or how much he has changed
he cannot be released

Another Tray

Sitting down to eat one day
same place, same food, same tired tray

to eat to live another day
to live to eat, I cannot say

to suffer and our debt to pay
so we can be released one day

and come back for another tray
and come back for another tray

THIS IS NOT

This is not a poem
It's not a sonnet
It's not a written piece of verse

It's not a prose inscription
arranged poetically
It's not an essay of few words

It's just an origami
handcuff key
no folding required

Floyd E. Kohn
Ghetto Ashes

I sucka stroke my blunt smoke, I French
roll my personality, then I blow it out.
Out, out to infect the "Any" unaffected.
The naughty boy, Sam Smith result of an
                    "open" kiss
                    on the mouth of man.
Black on crack crime, the blackbird
heard of Brokeback. That mountain
top is hard to climb, but once again it
is our time. Factory smoke, penitentiary
hope, I hope I choke for you every day. I'm
high off the memory of being free with
you one day. My order of the Phoenix
is the leanest bird, born again from
the Highland Project ashes. I am
possessed by a critical mess. Intestine
exhilaration is my bubble guts
nervous romantic companion, two
life forms and forms of time. The times
                    of us two longing
                    to be in tandem.

                              Discussions of you
                    with myself are never
                              random. Brain waves
are what I pass 'em. . . Inhale my thoughts,
warm like creamy espresso, undercurrents
careful not to avoid sin, overnight
invitation say let's do it again. This
femme fatale comes to you in all see-
through chainmail. All hail safe

awkwardness and on point pure bliss.
Saving "Graces" in the arms of your ruptured
bounty, in the arms of your many faces,
but I know every last one. We burn
affirmation down to the advantage
                or ask until
this encounter is a ruin of times past
blowing over a champagne glass. You have
brought to me the only dream that's ever
meant anything to me, sorry MLK,
but, there was another way for me
to be free at last. Born again from
the ashes, I am possessed by a critical mess.
Exhilaration is my romantic companion,
two lifetimes longing to be in tandem. Discussions
                of you
                with myself
                are never random
Brainwaves are what I passss 'em

Dell Konieczko
Besides Guilt, What, in Prison, is Mine?

Hope is the thing with feathers—

Oh. Sorry, Emily. Of course, that's yours, not mine.
Besides guilt, what, in prison, is mine?
This collection of objects?
Letters or photographs, perhaps?
Here's one of my mother.
I was thirty-four when we met.
No, she's not mine. She never was.
I bought this TV through the prison store;
It has my number engraved on it.
Thirteen rectangular inches offering me, in color,
A daily barrage of lifestyles
and life's accumulations that, apparently,
If I'm to be happy,
I just cannot do without—
But, of course, will never have.
I did buy it, though.
And the convict code says I should defend it to the death.
Would I? If it was stolen, would I
avenge its honor? Would that make it mine?

Hope is the thin—

I know, I know.
But guilt has feathers, too, Emily.
And it's not content with perching.
Like a frenzied cuckoo, it burrows
Inside the nest of my skin
With its jagged, quenchless beak agape,
It sucks down every cell that holds me
Together, that bands you to the thought
That you might be human;

That I might possess something in prison
Besides my blamable past.

The Heartbeat of the People, I am Told

(The Drum—The Drum
  The Drum—The Drum)

The Drum is the Heartbeat of the People, I am told.
Supposedly, it connects today's Anishinaabek to their ancestors;
to a tribal body that doesn't mind having maple in its veins
            and birchbark for skin;
that knows how to survive between the before and after.

I am told that it beats a rhythmic history
through the lives of a worthy people;
recounting in proud, systolic thumps
the details of a unique heritage.

I am told that if I listen carefully
I will hear, inside myself,
the Heartbeat of the People calling,
urging me to reclaim stewardship of Turtle Island;
to re-engage the enemy on a modern front—
in the schools, the boardrooms, the courts—
            and fight to belong.

(The Drum—The Drum
  The Drum—The Drum)

So, I close my eyes, I cover my ears, I stop breathing,
            and I listen and listen
            and listen—
I listen through the reservations, assimilation policies,
the abandonments and adoptions.
I listen through the ignorance and self-doubt.

I listen with every cell in me wanting to hear,
straining to hear, dying to hear even
the slightest murmur from the Heartbeat of the People.

And when I can no longer hold my breath

I realize that, although born a son of this land,
I am an orphan,
and the Heartbeat of the People will not beat for me.

Diana Lewis
Pinball People

I feel like my brain is drowning—
In a sea of emotional salt water
Tied up in mental seaweed
The food to my lifeline
And hope for my new future
Is ebbing and flowing
In a volcano of ideas that
Silently slip down a drain
Then erupts from its mountain!
Only to burn away into ashes that…
Get lost in the wind or harden into molten lava as they hit
The cooler temperatures of the earthly air
Ever-present in my mind,
Yet forgotten over time
As execution of "ideas" become
Landmarks upon which foundations built of
Ice are born; only to melt away
With the rising sun
Yet "inspiration" comes again, in warm rays
As the breeze caresses my face
And gently entices my body
I will follow its seductive whispers
Until I lose it to shadow
Or am lured away into—
The darkness by its brother
Finding new journeys into its depths
Only to explore something "different"
As I bounce off another wall like
A "pinball"
PEOPLE.

Justin Monson
Princes of Ennismore

-for Scott

Indulge me, my friend:
      How often do you recall the hours we once shared
      in the dusk of our younger years—
           the days we plucked
           that created my capture?
Those mid-summers when our faces held smooth.
      To be young was crucial
but to be us—Oh! To be us. . .
      brought waves of rapture upon fresh shores.

To our peers we were Dylan
in the aftermath
of courting electric:
      booed   but still followed, for our movements
      belonged to a less diffident time,
a time more littered with roads less traveled.
Alas, we were stuck:
      wading riotous waters, river currents
      shooting us into close deltas

Chanting tongues
the language of young outlaws
we held church in the depths of the dust—
ridden garage, weighed our youth on square digital scales.
Paper for product,
          paper for product,
               product for paper.

Onward the empire marched blind.
I still contend that half our money
touched the palms of Kevin at the Corner Store.
      who would we now be absent his ever-present Bluetooth
      his backwards flat brim and penchant for liquor
      sales to us neighborhood princes?

We poured lemon drops
        of half-truths into wanting ears
until quotas were filled
        or lips became puckered
only dropping stutters
        once whiskey dens dissolved
        within our light bones.

Thick nights we lit prayers in dank air
each breath came with the stench of galaxy
the sound of light-years penetrating the moon
until sleep interrupted a madness
in our lungs
the blood in our eyes
our lions in small cages of rib bone.

We roamed acid fields
in the still breath of Tiki torches
        volleyed bursts of laughter
into an Upstairs Room none were sure existed
from the back porch known to bestow histories.
The bleeding sky brought death to stars
        though we stole kayaks
        to cordon Dawn's physics.

To cut through Lake Oakland
in the slight trickle of morning
must be foreign to most.
        For in those lapels of lake
we spotted creases of infinite sky
        and we knew we had found
what we still search for;
I'd bet my life those slices of water
        remain.

I'd bet my life.

Daily we caught each other reaching
for that rebellious brand of freedom:

once arcing, found nothing
comes much free.
For we all learn that youth
        dies, or at least lies dormant.

L. Parker
something about the rain

There's a closeness i feel, when the icy drops caress my skin, but there's no chill. The anguishes of the heart i constantly feel, Pains deeply set, Even those the rain begins to heal. It's cold, it's wet, it's bland, but i'm affectionate toward this weather that i don't yet completely understand. Could it be the way it blurs my vision and makes me feel safely hidden from this colorless prism. Prisoned away for my impulsive decisions. The rain veils the fact i've yet to live up to my own ambitions. As the steady downpour beats the pavement and makes it glisten, i let the sound drown out the voices that eagerly beg me to listen. They scream they yell they try to convince me i'll never make it. So i grasp hold to my dreams lest they get it and break it. There's something unique about the noise, the way it conducts a light melody with the heavy drumming of its voice. There's something very odd, yet so very unique. Something about the calm it creates and sends us into a wonderful sleep. There's something about the rain, something i don't quite understand. Something i wish to carry everywhere i go, but i can't quite grasp it in my hand.

The ABCs of the Black Standard

Asinine assassins insidiously aspiring to asphyxiate the African aborigine. Amoral arrogant assailants amused with amplifying amphetamines in afflicted and appalling areas where African ascendency abides. Astounding amounts of arrant animosity aimed arrogantly casting aspersions with asperity on aristocrats and commoners apt to arise. Agitated apes apparently ascribing our absence of an apt apology on our automatic abhorrence of assimilating and being Americanized. Bullied, bludgeoned and burdened with burdensome bulks bent backward but never broken. Bigoted backbiters bent on blackballing blacks and bilking brothers with beclouding bills. Bound black brothers bravely bunched in the boats' bilge reeking of bilious bitter bile. Black bucks bucking because the branding burns. Blindfolded, bridled and bled by blond bloodletting bonafide bugbears. Burglarized, bought, botched, bootlegged and brought buck-naked in brash burgeoning bundles. Caught, chained, chafed and ceremoniously chastened. Cautioned to cease and cede control of our cerebral cavities. Curiously contemplating catholicism and christianity. Chasing a critical channel to cheat the cynical charlatan and control his catastrophe. Cold creatures created to infiltrate cracks in our African creed. Crazed criminals cramming cowardice into the coy, credulous and crass whilst crediting their cruelty to a criminal craft.

The Stone Speaks

As I lay here focused on life's issues, i begin to think.
What if these stone walls began to speak?
I wonder to myself what they'll have to say.
And would it even be something i'd heed?
Or would i simply pretend it hadn't said anything?
As i lay in this dark place wondering,
it sounds as if my cell begins to breathe.
i try and convince myself no life exists in this concrete.
But just as i begin to calm, the walls call out to me.
Impossible i think, "NO" the interrupting wall screams.
"This is not a dream."
Certainly the walls are mistaken, i think.
Walls made of stone could never speak.
"Pinch yourself and you'll see
That you're mine, and mine to keep.
A prisoner held within me
And a prisoner you'll always be."
One glance at the door, i wish now more than ever i had a key.
i've been here six years and it was only supposed to be three.
And as if my thoughts were perceived,
the walls made of stone smile with glee!
Over and over the wall begins to repeat,
"A prisoner held within me
And a prisoner you'll always be."
Despair begins to take me, as the wall repeats it convincingly.
Patiently i've been waiting for them to see
i am no longer the criminal i used to be.
For this it seems like i've been waiting an eternity.
For now i'll lie down to sleep
As the wall repeats,
"A prisoner held within me
And a prisoner you'll always be."

Steven Pribbernow
My Love, the Tempest, and the Chain Gang
An Erasure of Robert Frost's "A Line-Storm Song"

the line tattered and swift
is forlorn all day
quartz stones lift
and vanish away
the roadside too wet
expend in vain
over the hills
and in the rain

less to say for themselves
in the world's despair
these numberless years
they are no less
crushed by some
wild easily shattered
come be my love
where the rain blows

there is the urge
singing down
the shallow wind
from which to gather
if we go clear west
and come through dry
wilding
the rain-fresh

this whelming wind
seems like the return
to lands left
before the age of doubt
love came amain
into the storm
my love

An Alice State of Mind

Fall
down the
rabbit hole
to a place where
time and space collide
and shatter all we know.
Misconceptions turn into
us thinking we know about all.
Which, in itself, is a misconceiving.
Bound by our reality's restraints,
we're truly just misguided saints.
Are we really plunging down
to the abyss of naught?
Or are we confined,
suspended in
a bastille,
tightly
held?

Tripping Over Mushrooms on the Way Home

Cracked window panes stare outward vacantly.
Great holes overflow with sewage in the streets.
Lawns groan sickly everywhere, crying out in their
need for nourishment. This place of my youth is dead.
It has seen the fare cost this world extrudes from us all.
Wild hoarse herds of people stumble about, stuck in
the weakly routine The Machine forces them in.
Oh how it chews their choices, causing them to
bored up their lives to change. The who, what, when,
and wares they're charged with become everything.

Hear the things that will save me are gone,
and I came to be saved. To pare myself with
a past that fragmented long ago. To find that lost
peace of myself, not to become a gear in The Machine.
I will not be led down the path of the vein. The
rains of hope will guide me forward, pulling at me if
I stray, keeping me on my coarse journey. And, though
the souls of my shoes are weary, I will not be
waited down by a lack of conviction. A loan in this
world, I will find myself before I return Home.

I Cry

I'm just laying here
it's almost morning now.
I've been thinking all night
trying to figure this out.
I remember what you
once said to me:
"Stop holding it all inside.
That's no way to heal a heart.
Sometimes to feel better
first you must fall apart."

So I close my eyes and cry.
Softly,
as the tears roll down.
Lightly,
wishing you were here right now.
I hold my knees to my chest,
crying so coldly,
silently, lonely.
Wanting someone to hold me,
I just look up at the sky
and I cry.

Today is just another day
but I can't seem to smile.
So I sit out by myself
and just look around.
The world passes by me
without a single glance.
I could stay here forever
but I can't sit out this dance.
The days may be getting harder
but they're all just another to get through.
I know it'll be okay
because I'll do what you told me to.

So I close my eyes and cry.

Softly,
as the tears roll down.
Lightly,
wishing you were here right now.
I hold my knees to my chest,
crying so coldly,
silently, lonely.
Wanting someone to hold me,
I just look up at the sky
and I cry.

I'm staring up at the stormy night,
on the roof beside my window,
wishing I could fly.
You told me to let go sometimes,
to let my emotions out.
That, when you don't cry,
that's not what being strong's about.
Right now I'm falling over,
I just can't hold back this pain.
I take that step and plunge
out into the rain.

I cry.
Like the rain of the storm
as it's coming down.
Over thunder and lightning,
hidden in the dark.
I cry my last breath
and I fall apart.
I woke up this morning
to the sunshine of today.
I remembered what you told me
and I know I'm here to stay.
Because each day may be harder
to wake and face the light
but, darling, you showed me how
I can survive the night.

I cry. . .

The King Crow Has Plucked Out My Eyes

Alas,
       I am alone,
              floating in Darkness.
Caw! Caw!

I am alone,
       floating in Darkness,
              afraid,
Caw! Caw!

Floating in Darkness,
       afraid,
              I have a thought.
Caw! Caw!

Afraid
       I have a thought:
              Am I truly alone?
Caw! Caw!

I have a thought:
       Am I truly alone?
              Breath brushes the nape of my neck.
Caw! Caw!

Am I truly alone?
       Breath brushes the nape of my neck.
              I think now.
. . . Caw!

Rik
Debris

Sordid details—long vague.
Passed fog missed its calling.
Ship run aground.
I am the Captain.
I was at the helm.
"Lookouts to the conning tower. . ."
Still Faits—Ill-fated,
Built in Ireland,
sunk in America.
No Titanic.
Just me.
Rusting hulk discovered at depth.
Cast off pieces of me found
Speculation amongst the wreckage.
The once proud, now lay shattered.
Ghosts of the debris field.
A boot so ghastly, found, by named luggage,
broken artifacts of life ended.
The journey never finished
Shall I rise, to ride once more cursed waves?
Shall I become a relic—
rusting ruin of a bygone day?
Hope rode with me once,
Hope rides yet again.
So much to be done,
so much to rebuild.
So many missing parts
still remain in the debris field. . .

The Sun is Dead

Such a small thing,
so diminutive the gestures,
manners, common courtesy.
So, matter-of-fact, genteel.
Walk away with grace, poise.

So much, no longer.
Winds of time remember.
Quiet breezes blow spanish moss willows.
Sun dress in the grass,
Gloves on the hood, hat too.

Now I remember that sweet drawl.
Green eyes, soft smile, black hair shining.
I forgot you. . .
Shock me; how could I forget?
Grits, fried mushrooms and sweet wine. . .

I fall back to reset mode.
I forgot you on purpose.
I have to, or I can't recover.
So far away from green eyes,
gloves on the hood, hat too. . .

Memories fill my dreams, and I drift back. . .
Honest grits, no one made them like you.
I remember, I remember them,
                          and you
                               once. . .

Cadence, prose, poem. . .
She was there. . .
She lit within my life.
I watched her fold laundry,
she didn't know
              I loved her.

She stood in the sun, blouse blowing,
Hair shimmering,
>   yeah, I loved her.
Washing walls,
chasing the dog,
shopping for dinner,
paying the bills,
>   the more I saw,
>   the more I know
>   I loved her. . .
Awful, horrible, tragic. . .
>   wrenched away;
She lay amongst the shattered glass and twisted steel.
"It was an accident. . ." so the papers said. . .
Cold dirt, rain, the willows wept. Family in black.
>   flowers wilted, life never more. . .
They buried her
>   and killed the sun. . .
>   I died too. . .

Seven Scott
Inspired Mind

Startled from a dream, I woke in the night;
abuzz in my mind, I wrote in dim light:
  "Spare a thought for the ignorant man,
    for he knows not what he does,
  walking through life somnambulant
     'cause he sees not where he goes."
I bethought myself, What can this mean?
  Inspired mind by divination,
   or Bible passage I had once seen?

Gnawing at my gut I felt an unease;
peering at my plate, I wrote using peas:
  "Spare a thought for the hungry man,
    for with his eyes he would feast,
  rooting scraps from the garbage can,
     brought to live thus like a beast."
I bethought myself, What can this mean?
  Inspired mind through agitation,
   or homeless vet's sign I had once seen?

Raising wine to lip, I sensed something new;
I wrote in fresh snow with a yellow hue:
  "Spare a thought for the thirsting man,
    for he yearns to drink of life;
  in vain, he fills his leaking can,
     as he strives to slake his strife."
I bethought myself, What can this mean?
  Inspired mind in contemplation,
   or bumper sticker I had once seen?

Penned up quite some time, I loathe the wire fence;
to share its impact I rhyme in the present tense:
  Spare a thought for my jailor man,
    though he cares not what you think;
  if you ask me, this convict can
     spin the yarns to make you blink!"

I bethought myself, What can this mean?
I tire of my imprisonment,
and pine for the man I had once been!

Pressed Flowers

It's my earliest memories which most often
spring to mind,
           a wondrous variety of endurable forget-me-not
pressed in the dog-eared, yellowing pages of a favored novel,
           kept through the years to remind me
of that time before
           he was no longer there. . .

Glints on the pond butterfly kisses of sun.
Zephyr breathing his warmth through the dandelion fuzz.
Legs folded Indian-style
           in my fourth summer,
patient and watchful,
           another stone on the bank,
cane pole in a death grip,
           mouth watering. . .

The moment he carried me atop his shoulders,
my own private Atlas with me as his world,
no burden to him
           his first-born son.
My spirits hopping
           among the cottontail bunnies floating above,
those dizzying heights
           I've so rarely achieved.
The moment I learned to bait the hook,
squirming and red-faced at the puking worm,
peals of boyish giggles at my ineptitude,
           eyes wide to my father's deftness,
surprised by the force in the strike,
           alive to the fight in the fish. . .

I remember another image distorted by my flowing tears,
my mother bruised and disappearing into the corner,
him blaming her for what
           I can't now recall.
I remember the phone flying off the wall,

him storming out through the blackness of the apartment door,
the absentee years
                that drunkenly stumbled in after. . .

Knuckles whitened on these prison bars,
                I'm left to wonder why these old hurts
suffer me again and again
                to uproot them, like dead flowers.
Perhaps it's so I'll not
                commit the same mistakes,
or that I may somehow
                finally forgive him.
Either way, I press these flowers with an understanding
that nothing past accurately predicts the future,
particularly when it just wants to live in the present.

Dawan Smith
Girl I Didn't Know

Whoa, a girl I didn't know, uh-uh

She had a pretty smile, I mean some pearly white teeth
and she wore designer shades looking so jazzy.
Her 'do' was so laid, not a hair out of place
I said, "I gotta make sure this woman see my face."
I didn't sweat her too quick because she just came in,
I let her order something to eat and let chat with her friend.
This was my first time coming out to a jazz club
and I couldn't believe that might've been falling in love.
I stayed in the back trying to be discreet
But I was so mesmerized by those pearly white teeth.
Her friend talked a lot and she never looked my way
but the lights were kind of dim so that made it okay.
I wanted her attention so I started to think
I said, "I won't be average and send her a drink."
That's when I told the band to play something smooth
and dedicate it to the woman sitting at Table 2.

Whoa, girl I didn't know, uh-uh

I didn't say which one and that was by design
'Cause it was only two ladies and they both were fine.
Her girl was kind of flattered, so she looked around
but mine was kind of shy, she just put her head down.
That turned me on more, man, I can't even lie
to see this sexy young woman had the nerve to be shy.
A few guys approached and didn't get any play
and I even seen a few send some drinks their way.
But they didn't get mad when they got turned down
I said, "This is a smooth club, man I like this crowd."
Wasn't no sense in me sitting there dreaming of love
so I had to let her know who her admirer was.
But I had to do it in a way that was just right
So I chose to take advantage of that open mic.
I said, "This is for the sexy woman at Table 2

'cause I had to let you know that I'm admiring you."

Whoa, girl I didn't know, uh-uh

I put it down real smooth, everyone was surprised
they didn't know what to expect coming from the new guy.
When I got off stage everyone was shaking my hand,
that's when I knew I came up with a cold-blooded plan.
Another woman slipped me card and said, "You're alright,
if it don't work out with her you can call me tonight."
But I went to Table 2 and looked her right in the face
and said, "Hey, pretty lady, did you save me a space?"
She was still so shy that she didn't even speak
her friend moved to the side and said, "Here, have a seat."
Her friend wasn't shy about speaking her mind,
'Cause she said right then, "Girl this one is fine. . ."
We talked a little while, she started opening up
and passersby couldn't believe that I had such luck,
knowing she was feeling me, so I grabbed her hand
and said, "Come on, pretty lady, let me have this dance."

Whoa, girl I didn't know, uh-uh

She held on to my hand all the way to the floor
and then she whispered in my ear saying, "Please stay close,
and there is something about me that I think you should know,
is that I never had a dance with a man before."
I said, "I'm glad I'm the first and I hope I'm the last."
She said, "You got a lot of charm and you even got class.
Most guys talk to me because they think that I'm fine,
But they always walk away when they find out that I'm blind."

"Whoa! Girl I didn't know, uh-uh. . .
but it won't change a thing."

Dominique C. Stone
W.R.I.T.E. (When Reality Is Too Evil)
-a paradelle for Demitrious

Wake up, Write, no time for Sleep.
Wake up, Write, no time for Sleep.
Spit Funk waves upon the Soul of the Pistons
Spit Funk waves upon the Soul of the Pistons
Wake up, no time for the Piston Funk.
Write, Spit waves upon the Soul of Sleep.

Flare the Spinach sticks to clear the Hurdles of Bluto
Flare the Spinach sticks to clear the Hurdles of Bluto
Allow Organized noise to set The Mood
Allow Organized noise to set The Mood
Bluto Mood Flare Allow noise to Set
Organized sticks of Hurdles the Spinach clear.

W.R.I.T.E. Push your pen
W.R.I.T.E. Push your pen
At all cost, Till your Intellectual Property
At all cost, Till your Intellectual Property
Push your Intellectual pen
W.R.I.T.E., till At all your Property cost.

Allow time to sleep, wake up
W.R.I.T.E. and hurdles of Bluto
Set the mood, flare the spinach sticks
Till your soul clear. Push the pen for
Intellectual funk waves, spit upon organized
Noise, and to Property of Pistons. At all cost, write.

Michael Sullivan
The Germophobe's Dilemma

when one finger touches another
how long do you have
to wash your hands

or for

finger and thumb gestures
mixed phalangeal clasping and shaking
full frontal fist bumps

during

the great plague
of door knob cooties

Grrr
(told in nice words)

When the uniformed state employee did me dirt one time too many
I said to him, when he was with a gaggle of his kind:
Mr. —, Darn you, darn your dog!
Could this be disrespectful, you stupid whelp of a female dog!!
He wrote me a citation saying I was majorly in the wrong place
When I got the paper, I told him:
Keister thy deity, feces worshiper!!!
After that, he looked out for me some
But usually left me alone
Maybe, I should have kept my mouth shut
But, Gosh darn the dirty dog!!!
Gosh darn it all!!
Bow wow!
Woof woof

bug boy

when you mess with someone somehow
small—to play big
all you have done is
pull the legs off bugs

each bug has 6 legs and 4 wings
10 ways to pretend you're a man
boy—a foolish baby boy
man up—don't do it

Daniel Turrentine
Spending Time Without You

I knew you
in a time
where seconds ceased
to count down
our remaining moments

shared in a bliss-filled
present
previous the melting wax
struggle to walk and breathe
now

where time stands still
in an uncomfortable
silence kind of disturbance
you know the kind of time
I mean

where your skin feels foreign
and familiar strangers
escort you through
their insecurities
carefully projected as your faults

because without you
seconds cease to be kind
and this is time
doing its best to be unkind
in a place, where you cease to be

Dennis Vesey
The African American Evolution

I've been frozen solid longer than a glacier
Hundreds of years before my mother's first menstruation
When I wasn't even a thought, just the hope of battered and beaten,
but not broken slaves

I began to thaw somewhere near the Everglades
But hypothermia travelled with me for a century
No feeling in my fingertips, so I never could get a handle on success
You would think that would have caused me to blow my cool
But I'm so cold, I done navigated my way through hell, shook the
devil's hand, and
       still never reached my boiling point
You wonder how I did it, well, my soul's a jolly giant, with a vantage
       point that
Allows me to see the forests through the trees, as well as the stem
on each and every leaf

My future's brighter than the Arizona sun
If God knew the heights I planned to reach, he'd change each and
       every last one of our tongues
I'm heaven bound, but fully thawed, gravitated 6,000 miles above
       the surface
At this altitude, I'm responsible for global warming

My ultraviolet shine derives from my natural energy source that
       makes me a star
with rays that stray from freefall space down to the lithosphere
Damn it I'm here! I'm there, I'm everywhere, and somewhere in
       between
walking low as roaches, but also soaring as high as the carbon atom

Just focus your optical lens in my direction and you'll see
I poured my thoughts into a bottle, called it hip hop, and gave the
       world a sip
Now I reside in every medulla oblongata, from the Alps to the
       Congo

I'm leader of the free world, the slave has become a king
I'm charcoal broiled, but still as cool as a glass of lemonade
The insistency of one's persistency
towards violence
permeates through the air

From the malformed minds
of Neanderthals
who refuse to grow beyond
early evolutionary paradigms
of an acceptable social design

That predates the now
by millennia
and years of philosophical struggle
seems a wasted thought

In moments of hate
when the beast of senseless rage
is released and allowed to play
we lose all
that we've striven for
yearned, burned, and died for

In an instant
we are back
marveling over fire
and considering
the limitless possibilities
of the wheel

Joseph Villarini
Time for a Change

Sometimes, I wonder if my lyrics are powerful enough
to move the masses. Or am I too passive?
Are my words heartfelt?
Does it matter if I can make a woman's heart melt
when I left so many women heartbroken?
My grandmother used to say we were born Kings,
but how can Kings be born into poverty?
The first money we see
comes from playing Monopoly,
we're living in houses, but we don't
own property, kids that I grew up with
weren't educated properly.
But I graduated and still ended up
in prison for armed robbery.
I guess we all had the wrong philosophy, fast money
put us on a fast track to a jail cell
and a quick glimpse of hell.
You wouldn't believe the things I've seen,
exposed to the darkest sides of the human being,
but what can you expect when they've taken
our humanity, the strongest men are on the verge
of insanity. Dear Mama, this ain't the man
I planned to be, I was judged by one man, I think
I stand unbroken. I was once a blind man, now
my eyes are wide open. My voice speaks for the
oppressed so they won't die hopeless.
They're stuck in the cage but not stuck in
a criminal mindframe. We should be uplifting our
brothers and raising our kids the right way instead
of raising the crime rate, otherwise
there's no hope for the future, and the truth
hurts. If you don't feel these nouns and verbs,
I guess, you don't get the subject.

Cozine Welch
On Top of Gray

In a highrise on Jefferson Street,
a deluxe apartment in the sky,
my young eyes watch tired muscles struggle
to move the rickety metal tubes my mother uses
to help her walk.
Insectoid and otherworldly to my imaginative eyes
they click and clack like mandibles
folding out and in and out again
never bending or buckling but
with every motion giving the terrifying impression
of impending collapse.
My mother's legs trail behind in an unsteady step,
effort etched across her face in a frown of determination.
I look from her legs to mine and wonder why
we can't trade for a while. I'll share.
Though I don't know how these baby-fat kneecaps
could help, really. But maybe
when mine are big and strong like Daddy's.
He can pick her up, carry her around.
I'm just short and chubby and have to get out of the way.
Daddy puts his finger in my belly button and I laugh.
Mommy doesn't smile when she uses her walker
but she smiles for me when I come forward, tentatively,
afraid the walker will "snap!"
and eat my fingers if I get too close.
I look up at her beaming face
and somehow I know mommy had to climb high,
high above the pale grey fog that settled about her countenance,
high above the sad, drab pigment of plastic
pressure-molded handgrips,
high above the sorrow covered crests of this
mountain of medical machinery,
high above all that would bring her down
just to present me that loving bit of sunshine.
The effort makes her shoulders heavy, makes her
seem to sag under the weight of it all.

Later in life I would find it strangely "coincidental"
that mama got multiple sclerosis, that she got sick
once she got pregnant with me;
Son. Harbinger.
But not today. Not yet.
Now I play with the walker when no one sees,
when it is not alive. I climb it, hang from it,
try to use it like she does. I press metal buttons
that resist and rebuff my touch,
needing to understand its power, to unlock its secrets.
Why is it necessary? Why does it have to be here?
I stare at my warped reflection on its rounded
metallic surface and watch my nose grow bulbous as I
sweep back and forth and side to side in hypnotic sway.
Cloud banded sunlight from the balcony lends an
even more ashen pallor to the gray steel.
I climb atop and look out, down at the city,
and down at the sky, from here
on top of gray

Spectrophobia

I fight
to deprogram what's been encoded
I need more than the
regular ration that's been
forced into me
from this stockpile of miseducation
they've stored for me.

I fight
to ignore what's been
bored into me.
It's given so little.
I need more from me.
Please.

Brainwash my thoughts.
Remove a stain
so that a new one may lay
where the previous had lain.
Exchange
one frame of reference for another,
one prejudice for another,
one seed of hate for its asexual mother.
Same lame
low self-esteem fear extreme.
Ultra-Conservative / Left-Wing radical.
Neo-Nazi / Black National
Cut, copy, paste, and send the rational
on extended sabbatical.
Right thinking has no listing
in this
emotional catalog.
There is no reason for reason to be
in this
powder-keg. So
make a power-pledge.

"I pledge allegiance to blind obedience.
To allow pain, anger, and pride to rise above my reason.
To allow the peace of my greeting
to be replaced by a hatred seething,
cleaving what is humane
from the core of my humanity."

I fight
to control the
misguided man in me,
to subdue the subjugator.
I fight,
only to become
what I have conquered.

Gray Skies Up Ahead

A collection of specimens
defined by grievance
drifting through the spaces
we've placed in between us

I look from these men
up towards the sky
and see similarity.

The clouds seem to move
faster than the distance they've travelled
tells me is possible.
I watch men do the Level IV shuffle
outside my window,
a stratagem where prisoners use
measured steps to extend their time
in the sun,
to extract recreation from destination,
from a walk,
and I see the same:
Heaven and Earth reflecting.

In watching
I sometimes forget the obvious, like how
we all wear the same thing.
So different we seem to my eye.
Special,
each from the other.
It's always hard to reconcile that
emotion
with the oft-enforced fact
of an identity reduced to a number.
The marvel of man, that.

Just last night another faceless number
hung himself
here

in Administrative Segregation.
A stormcloud releasing rain.
A downpour!
He just wanted to leave.

Prepossessed

Ill fitting prison issue shirts
complete with
orange-colored construction crew stripes
and deep, plunging V-necks
exposing collarbone and bosom
Steps made in
staggered ankle-chained increments
Slave shuffle
Ankles rubbed raw from
unyielding steel
made stainless so that blood
wipes off easily
Wrists and waist bound
together, base and tether
bellychains leave arms
stiff in robot pose
Natural swing halted, natural motion
froze; A reminder to not even bother
to grow
I see my reality with memory superimposed:
An old N.W.A. video
The camera is flickering, a
switch back and forth
from slave to prisoner,
slave
to prisoner
while an old soulman's sampled voice sings
"express yourself"
Damn
times change
but relations stay the same
No Dr. Dre and
no Ice Cube to the rescue,
this scene plays
to its conclusion
unnoticed,
unfilmed,

and un-
important

Your life only
matters
when the camera's on

Chum

White flecks
discarded with disdain
prim painted fingers
brush my shoulders with well-bred haughtiness
instinct argues against intent
with elbows bent
high society feigns to lift
low morale
with lower morals
prints of Burberry, the scent of Dior at my table
signposts of the newly able
lips lacquered in a taunting hue
provoking, vexing,
arousing
Knuckles of brass wrapped in hands of lambskin
throw knife points over champagne flutes
I walk the path of daggers
my practiced nimbleness perfected
countless dry-runs, rehearsals and performances
prime my code-switching character for
private shows wherein
private shows public personas to be
oiled images craftily set atop
grotesque canvas
I dance this river of revulsion under
beads of sweat
under
water but not wet
casting about for a life preserver
I know what's next
know how this ends
circled by fins.

The Docent Lecturer

(Professor) He creates the
aura, he delivers
with spontaneity
of a freestyled free verse but with
the quality and substantive substance
of what's been well rehearsed.
(Student 1) How does he do it?

He writes
with focused thought
A particle beam of poetic particulars
imparting their imprint upon
recycled fibrous modern papyrus
through
ballpoint pen with pinpoint accuracy
laughingly laying ink trails
to be followed like
heat signatures from his signature salvo.

(Student 2) So does he freewrite or rewrite or both?
(Professor) Method here is irrelevant because either way,
once you hear it or read it you immediately see that
you're wrong, he's right.
(Student 1) Wait. What?
(Student 2) Then how does he do it?
He writes
like Theocritus in socks with scuffed, frayed cuffs
amongst the weak,
amongst us
Metrical homunculus
formed from amongst the dust
with sperm-like squirm
Black germ swimming past
past terms of identification, each one
void
His parents a pair-of-no-I.D.'s
so he was born a par-a-noID

Skipping schismatic
dualistic schizophrenic rites to get
schizy with the neophytes on an atypical Friday night
Lights, the electric hum
throbbing in sync with a spector's drum
the lecherous inhaling the sun with a leper's lung
"white lines" is being sung as
he has become a being
coming into his own and
as he recites his song you
realize
what you knew all along

You're wrong. He's right.
How does he do it?
He *writes*.

Tanya Willhelm
Where Are All the Flowers

"They say that life is what happens to you when you make other plans."
— Death

I awake trapped, can't breathe, can't see. My chest arises feeling
dirt pushing onto my chest. I start clawing at the ground. My hand
grabs hold of a root. I pull and the earth falls in. I instantly start
freaking out. Then I feel the air above. I push and claw my way
through the earth. I notice tied to my finger is a string that leads to
a bell without a clapper. I look around. I am in the Huron Valley
Complex prison graveyard. Next to me is Mrs. Stacey's grave stone
— a friend of mine who just recently passed away of a questionable
drug overdose of Geodon. Her grave now appears empty as if
someone has recently dug her up. I scramble and begin to run
through the forest as fast as I can. Heading away from the prison,
now knowing that someone in the prison is killing the women
and burying others still alive. Not paying attention I trip and fall
over a wire that's been hidden in the ground. A stick goes deeply
into my thigh. Blood sprays out but then stops, it must not have
hit an artery. I try to pull it out it hurts so bad. It comes out with
a sickly sucking noise. I notice then that the stick is covered with
leeches that are now in the thigh as well. I can feel them wiggling
around sucking my blood. I brace myself and begin the horrid task
of digging my fingers into my own flesh to pry the leaches out.
Amazingly it is warm and soft. I feel the first leach. I pull it out
and my mind tells me I need to put my blood back. So I have to
eat the leach, crunching it, yum. I suck and savor the taste, that's
when I look over and see, Mrs. Martinez and Lafountin standing
there watching me. I am no longer in the forest but in the infirmary
holding up a noodle as if it is a leach. I look around realizing now
that the room is full of flowers, family and friends.

Prose

Bill Cook
Chow Hall Derby

In twenty minutes the imminent call would come, just like it did yesterday and every day before and every day after this day. Guys begin gathering along the walls flanking the front doors. At first there are only a couple, those who have nothing more to do than wait in anticipation, but as time moves along more guys slowly drift in. A low murmur emanates from the small crowd. Just like stereotypical old-lady gossip, and the latest rumors are eagerly exchanged. "Did you hear about Country?"

"Who's Country?" one of the men asked.

"What about him?" came a reply from another.

The first speaker began to tell all he knew about the man named Country (who liked country music). Of course he embellished it to his liking.

Another person spoke to his neighbor standing next to him, "You heard about store didn't you?"

"What's up with the store this time?" came a quick response from somebody else.

"They're changing. . ."

"How about that Larry guy?"

"Which one?"

"You know. The one that plays the keyboard."

"What about him?"

"Well, he's. . ." The rest of the statement went unheard.

Roving eyes dart this way and that making sure the subject of the gossip is nowhere to be seen. Heaven forbid should he happen to appear and hear what's being said about him!

A little more than five minutes passed and already guys were standing shoulder to shoulder along both sides of the short hallway increasing the noise level to a low buzz. Interestingly, it always seems to be same ones doing all the talking, while the silent or soft spoken men stood quietly while anticipating the call. Of course, any word passed is nothing less than earth shattering, at least in the mind of the purveyor.

The corrections officers sit together in their small office paying little or no heed to what's being said outside their domain. The COs have much more important things to discuss and their own gossip to spread. Gossip is an integral part of prison life—some to be taken seriously, and some to be scoffed at.

It's now ten minutes before the call and everyone, except for the card players and a few other die-hards in the unit, are gathered at the doors. The buzz of conversation grows into an indecipherable cacophony of words and sounds. As the anticipation of the call grows, the guys begin shuffling around jockeying for position nearest the doors. Nervous feet stomp the floor not unlike a thoroughbred standing at the gate just before the start of the big race. Knowing the time was close, the buzz lowered to a monotonous din, each person having one ear tuned to the sound of the officers' two-way radio that would announce the call. The COs, still sitting at their desk, search for something unknown on the computer. From past experiences, they knew it was unwise to get in the herd's way, especially when the call finally came.

"SQUAWK!" The anticipated sound everyone was waiting for, the identifying sonance of the two-way radio, not unlike the bang of a starter's gun, resonated through the mass of humanity gather at the doors. Even before the call could be verbalized by a CO the doors suddenly burst open and the thrice-daily race to chow was on! All the talking came to an abrupt halt, and all energy became focused on the squeezing out through the doors and onto the open walkway. Speed was of the essence. Who was going to be first? Who was going to be last, and left in the dust?

"B-Unit. Send sides one and two to chow." The call came over the radio, but it mattered little now. Most of the horde had already pushed its way through the narrow entryway and out the double doors. Beyond the doors and into the open air the once tightly packed mass of humanity moved with surprising speed and quickly spread out.

THEY'RE OFF! Big Red (from his large size and flaming red hair and beard) is leading the surge, but Little John (also named for his large size) and M (the first letter of his first name) are rapidly closing the gap. Others, too numerous to identify, scurry ahead of the rest of the pack trying to maintain their closeness to the lead hoping to take over. Managing to force his way through the clogged open doors, Hustle-Man (he's always selling something on the yard) and his buddy Ray-Ray (a doubling of his first name, Ray) raced along the outer flanks of the moving mass. Running, of course, was grounds for a reprimand so only fast walk was in order. It's still anybody's race to see who will be the first to enter the chow hall a mere 75 yards away.

Here comes Green (his last name!) Green, nearly running, approaches and begins to pass M. M is having nothing to do with that! He immediately lengthens his stride and quickens his pace. Big Red turns his head to look back, and instantly sees some of the others rapidly closing the gap. THERE HE GOES! Looks like he put it in overdrive! If he can keep up the pace, nobody is going to catch him! By lengthening and quickening his stride, he blasts away from the pack.

It's getting down to the wire now! The chow hall is only a few yards away! All Big Red has to do is maintain his pace and he should be all right.

OH WOW! Could it be!? COULD IT BEEE!? Is that Li'l Bama sneaking through the crowd? He actually manages to wend his way through the mass like it was standing still. OH NO! There's BIG BAMA! (Both come from Alabama, but Big Bama is much larger in stature and Li'l Bama is much younger.) What's going to happen now?! WATCH OUT! Big Bama's extending his arm! OH MY GOODNESS! It caught Li'l Bama across the chest stopping him cold nearly knocking him off his feet. Grassman (he works on the yard crew and was always covered with cut grass) is taking advantage of the opportunity and catching up to his diminutive friend.

THERE THEY GO! Side-by-side Grassman and Li'l Bama quickly skirt around Big Bama's outstretched arm and are speeding away. It looks like they plotted a course of least resistance right through the middle of the crowd! Now they're making a beeline to the edge of the crowd where they could move more freely. Could this be their avenue for victory? The way is clear now! They're hurrying even faster than before! OH WOW! They caught up to, and are beginning to pass, the leaders. Big Red, though, looks determined to be first!

Only a few yards to go now! Looks like, and I'll give you 2-to-1 odds, Big Red is going to be first once again! BUT LOOK! Coming up quick is M and Little John. Hustle-Man has fallen back, but Grassman and Li'l Bama are coming on fast! They're almost right up front! Are they going to beat Big Red this time? LOOK! There's

Green! Apparently he has no desire to be left out and is hot on Grassman's tail. He's starting to go around. LOOK AT THAT! Li'l Bama just stepped in front and cut him off. OH NO! Green just shoved Li'l Bama! Good thing Grassman was right there to catch him. I'LL BE DARNED! It didn't even slow them up!

Big Read is there, and nobody's in his way, either! THERE HE GOES! He thrust out his arms and burst through the chow hall doors right in front of Grassman and Li'l Bama. HE MADE IT! HE MADE IT! BIG RED BEAT EVERYONE!

Since he was first through the doors, Big Red immediately chose the left serving line and moved up to the counter. Grassman and Li'l Bama came through the doors next going directly to the right serving line. Then, as all the others came through the doors the serving line grew until both extended outside beyond the doors.

The serving lines worked pretty fast, and the guys took their filled food trays to a table and sat down. With shifting eyes, they looked all around to make sure a CO wasn't eyeballing them. Satisfied they weren't being watched, they quickly took food from their trays and began stuffing it into their shirts, pants and socks. Of course, the COs watching them on the overhead security cameras find their "secret" stuffings quite amusing. With their clothing filled, and trying to look as innocent as possible, they get up and carry their empty trays to the disposal station. Another person immediately takes the vacated seat.

The drone of a couple of hundred men all talking at once fills the chow hall, making it difficult to hear anything beyond the table conversation. Numerous COs walk around acting as if they cared, but as long as there was not trouble to be had, most couldn't care less.

Not wanting to create a means to draw any unwanted attention, the walk back to the unit is slow and casual. Shirts, pants, and socks were stuffed to the max! Any more would be too obvious and would invite a search by a CO. Fear of losing everything to a wise CO was on everyone's mind. Later, after yard closed, the herd would jockey for position around the microwaves to carefully assemble and cook their imaginary gourmet feast to accompany an evening of TV entertainment.

Denver
Jimmy Hoffa—An Unsolved Mystery

He was 5 feet 5 inches tall and built like a fire plug. He had a full head of black hair that was just beginning to show gray on the sides. At 58 years old he could still bench press four hundred pounds. But his best feature was his radio announcer's voice. The minute you heard it, he had your full attention.

He was a bona fide big shot 12 years earlier. Robert Kennedy, himself, put him away in federal prison for 13 years. President Nixon pardoned him in 1971. The release stipulated that he would not participate in union activities until 1980. He was back. It was a long time until 1980, and he was building a groundswell to get back into the game.

It would not be easy. Frank Simmons was head of the unions now. He had a power base of his own. Simmons was connected with mobsters close to the organization.

On July 30, 1975, Jimmy Hoffa drove to the Red Fox Restaurant in Bloomfield Hills for a midday sit-down to quell a feud and discuss his future with the Teamsters. It was rumored, that local Mafioso Anthony "Tony Jack" Giacolone and New Jersey racketeer Anthony "Tony Pro" Provenzano were also at the meeting.

Hoffa did not return home from that meeting. His wife reported him missing the next day. His empty car was found in the restaurant parking lot by the police.

There has been much speculation over the years. Criminals trading information for reduced charges on pending crimes have had the fence looking all over Michigan—in the trunks of crushed cars, under a swimming pool in Bloomfield Hills, in the trunk of the Cadillac under a garage, and in a gravel pit in Highland. Other stories have surfaced that Hoffa is buried in New Jersey somewhere in Giants Stadium.

I have personally spoken with Giacolone, Joe Tocco, Joe Ruggirello and numerous other connected wiseguys. Here's the deal: nobody has a clue where Hoffa ended up. Nonetheless, several million dollars came up missing from the Teamsters Union pension fund. The money was never recovered. Hoffa never had a chance to spend it in prison.

Over the years one rumor has persisted and consistently

prevails. "Jimmy Hoffa took off for Brazil with a go-go dancer." It pops up every time the feds, and coincidentally the media, chase another "credible" lead and come up empty.

I will tell you a true story. This is not information to be peddled callously to the tabloids for a few extra zoo zoos and wham whams. This is my gift to you for being in a league of prison literature aficionados.

In 1979, I wrote an abbreviated history of the events inside Marquette prison. I conferred with an old con named Walt. Walt was nearly 80 years old. He was serving his second life bit. Walt had been in the Purple Gang back in his youth.

While collaborating on the history project, Walt opened up to me. He confided that he received a postcard every once in awhile from a big shot. He showed me a stack of postcards postmarked from Brazil. They were beach scenes with white sand, clear blue water, yachts and beach bunnies. They were all signed Big Jim. Walt transferred to the big yard in the sky a few years later. His postcards were probably destroyed with the rest of his property.

I never put it together until years later. The possibility was remote at best. In truth, I never even heard the rumor that Hoffa got to Brazil with a go-go dancer until the last big story where the fence dug up a farm in Troy, Michigan. I mean, without those postcards, it's just another incredible story about one of the world's greatest unsolved mysteries.

Scotty G
The Vault

I finally reach the bottom of the staircase and step onto the black marble tiles. The floor feels cool and smooth beneath my feet. There isn't much light, but I've been down here so many times I can find my way blindfolded.

After a short walk, I stand in front of the massive steel door. It towers over me like a benevolent guardian and seems to ask, "Are you sure you want to do this again?" In response to the silent question, I punch the security code into the keypad, stare unblinking into the retinal scanner, and speak their required phrase for the voice recognition system.

There is a short beat, followed by a metallic female voice saying "access granted." I hear well-oiled gears and precision mechanisms turning. Then, with a soft, sucking gasp, the rubber seals break and the huge door yawns lazily open.

I sigh as I step into the room, pause for a moment and close my eyes. I inhale a deep lung full of the triple-filtered, purified air, which is maintained at a perfect 65 degrees Fahrenheit and 32 percent humidity.

Impossibly, I imagine that I can detect a faint odor. A blend of sweet and sour scents. Like overripe fruit, like something good gone bad. I dismiss the thought as a product of my overactive nocturnal imagination.

The vast space is quiet apart from the background hum of a multitude of tiny cooling fans. Each of the chest-high display cases visible in the semidarkness has a sophisticated computer system in its base and the fans are there to prevent overheating.

I start my usual wander around the room, looking at the displays. I feel as if I'm browsing a museum, but I suppose that's a pretty accurate description of this place after all. Most of them I glide past, ignoring for now. Others catch my attention and I moved towards them, reliving the memories they hold in vivid, lifelike clarity simply by placing my hand on their biometric panels.

Over the years I have devised pet names for some of the displays. "Happy Meal" boxes are little packets of joy that I look forward to with childish glee, but the experiences they offer are over all too quickly, and I'm left feeling half-empty instead of half-full. Awkward and embarrassing scenes are found in the "Red Face" cases. Most of them I can laugh at now, the intervening years having softened their effect on me. I relive them with a wry smile on my face, as if I'm watching a movie where someone else is playing my part. If I'm roaming around and tears appear in my eyes, I know I must be getting close to one of my bittersweet "Onion Peel" memories. I need to be careful with those: Like many things in life, sadness can be addictive.

Some displays remain unnamed. I don't give them names because naming bestows power, and they already have more than enough power over me. Even though time and distance spend the gulf between then and now, I still wince at the rock pain they cause me. I know I should forgive myself, move on, and leave these memories behind, but knowing what to do and doing it are two separate things.

Inevitably, I find myself standing in front of my least favorite, most visited memory case. It is the largest in the room, and within its tinted glass, a bright red LED grows and fades repeatedly, pulsing out a subtle warning. One of these days I might take heed, but not this time. I move closer.

Unlike the other containers, the access path for this one is actually inside the case. As I approach, a previously invisible orifice appears on the front panel, inviting me to insert my hand. Without realizing that I'm doing it, I bite my lower lip and rub my right forearm.

Last chance. I could turn away now. I could walk out of the vault, go back upstairs and return to bed. I could watch TV, listen to music, or read a book. Hell, I could grab a beer from the fridge, sit on the porch, and gaze at the stars.

I do none of these things. The rational part of my brain acknowledges them to be perfectly reasonable and acceptable alternatives, but they are all crushed beneath the implacable weight of regret and voice in my head telling me I deserve this. With grim determination, I push my arm into the circular opening.

As soon as my hand touches the access pad, the LED changes to a malevolent green color and yet again I am startled by the sudden appearance of two things. First, my feet and ankles are secured by flexible, but unbreakable, plastic shackles. Second, the hole is now ringed with a dozen sharp metal spikes that curve inward, gently pricking my skin. I am reminded of the signs at some parking lot entrances: "Do not back up! Severe damage may occur!"

And suddenly I am immersed and flowing down a rushing river of memory, back to the pain and shame and wishing I could do things differently this time. Images, sensations and emotions course through me like a series of high-voltage electric shocks. The mental agony is so intense that I don't even notice the barbs digging into my arm, holding me in place.

After some time, I open my eyes. I am sweat-drenched and limp, swaying slightly back and forth. Beads of drying blood and circle my forearm. The LED has resumed its patience red blinking.

My feet, now free, shuffle me listlessly back to the vault door. I exhale loudly as I close it and reset the security system.

"Well," I say to myself, "It'll be a long time before I do that again!"

Of course, that's what I said last night.

Daniel Lee
Passenger

The rhythmic pitter-patter of the large rain drops smacking against the windshield mixed with the whoosh-whoosh of the windshield wipers is relaxing, like a lullaby to the man sitting behind the steering wheel. Matt's been driving this long, dark, empty, pothole-covered road for what feels like an eternity. His eyes grow heavy and he nods a couple of times before he pulls to the shoulder and slaps himself awake. A cold cup of coffee sits in the cup holder. He drinks it down in one long swallow—It does nothing. According to his directions it should only be about another hour before Matt gets to the woman's house who will rid him of his problems. "How can I stay awake?" he asks himself. He flips through the radio stations until he finds one playing nothing but heavy metal (his favorite genre). Matt turns the volume up so high it hurts his ears and causes an immediate headache. He puts the car into drive and presses down on the gas pedal. The tires spin and kick up gravel for a second before the tread catches and pulls him back onto the pavement.

Twenty minutes go by. Although he's still tired, the music keeps him from dozing off again. The volume goes low and the radio is turned to the oldies station. Matt looks to the passenger seat and the woman is smiling at him through dry, cracked lips. Her eyes are black. Looking into them is like looking into a dark abyss. Her pale skin is practically transparent. Long, flowing, dirty blonde hair hangs from her head in tangles. The dress she wears is in tatters. Although he couldn't see her, he knew she had been there the entire time. This is the problem that he's going to see Caroline, a self-proclaimed witch, to be rid of. He looks back at the road and tries to ignore her.

He doesn't know how this female apparition became attached to him, or where she even came from. He's noticed odd things, unexplainable things, happening for a long time now, but up until a year ago, she's never been visible. At first, he thought is was kind of cool; now, not so much. Until recently she's never caused him any harm, but she's become too attached now, even violent sometimes. Any time he has company, especially female company, she scares them away. Things get thrown, glass gets broken, he's been pushed, clawed and choked. She reminds him of a jealous girlfriend he had years before.

Matt wipes his brow, reaches down, turns the heavy metal station back on and the volume back up. Before he pulls his hand away he feels her grip on his forearm, her fingers searing into his flesh. "Let me go!" he screams at her. When he turns his head and looks at her, she winks at him and releases her grip, her smile turns to a scowl; she doesn't like this type of music. He leaves the heavy metal station on, pulls his hand away from the radio, looking at his arm he sees three long, dark scratches where she grabbed him. Once again, the oldies station is turned back on. This time he leaves it, thinking to himself, "What the hell. In a little while she'll be gone." He begins tapping his fingers on the steering wheel to the rhythm of Ben E. King asking his darling if she'll stand by him. Matt's content with this song, he's always liked it. Looking back at the passenger seat, he sees it's now empty.

His phone vibrates in his pocket and he pulls over and pulls the slim phone out. "Hello," he answers. "Hold on." It's his girlfriend, Amy. He opens his door and steps out of the car. Instantly the rain soaks him. He looks back into the car and sees her sitting there, staring at him. He slams the door. Amy asks Matt if he's been to see Caroline yet. "No. I think I'm almost there though." He pauses. "Love you. Bye" He hangs up the phone. The large drops mildly sting as they hit his open eyes. Matt walks down the road a little ways then reaches his hand into his pocket and pulls out a crumpled pack of Camels. He takes the last cigarette from the pack. It's broken. This pisses him off something awful. Matt's been saving this cigarette all night, and now that he needs one, he can't have it.

Suddenly, headlights shine on him from behind; this startles him and causes him to jump. Matt turns quickly on his heels and only sees his own car. For a second he thought another car was on the road, but there isn't. He stares at his little car through the bright headlights and can just barely make out the silhouette of the woman. He throws the broken cigarette to the ground, outstretches his arms high over his head and begins yelling "Fuck!" repeatedly as loud as he can until his throat becomes sore and his voice grows hoarse.

Matt gets back into the car and looks at the empty seat. "You're a real bitch, ya know that?" He then chuckles to himself. Water drips from his long brown hair. He runs his hand through it then turns the key over. As soon as the car comes to life, Led Zeppelin's "Stairway to Heaven" comes from the speakers. Immediately he turns the radio off. He puts the car into drive and pulls back onto the road.

A short time later he begins dozing again. He fights his way through it. Unexpectedly he feels something on his leg. Looking down he sees her hand resting there. Matt gives her a grimace and looks back at the road. Her hand stays put for a few minutes.

He comes to a busy crossroad, drives across, pulls over and calls Caroline to see how much further he has to go. Three rings then her phone's answered. "Hey, Caroline, it's Matt." He says into the phone. "Hold on, I need to put ya on speaker. I can barely hear you." He turns on the speakerphone. "How far till I get there?"

"Well—where are you now?" She asks, her voice raspy.

"I'm on Wilson, just passed Elms."

"Okay, another mile you'll pass Morrish Road; a little further up you'll go over a small bridge, then exactly half a mile after the bridge is my house, on the left hand side. You can't miss it." She pauses. "Is she—uh—is she with you?"

He looks to his right and sees the empty seat but knows that it's not really empty. "Yup." He glances into the rearview mirror then back to the passenger seat and sees her. She staring at him with a questioning look. "Yeah, she's here."

"Okay. Good," says Caroline. "See ya in a few minutes." The phone goes silent.

Pulling away, he feels her cold hand gently grasp his. Lightly her fingers rub across his. Matt knows she's pleading with him. His sixth sense is telling him that she knows what's about to happen. "Sorry. It has to be done." He looks at her again and sees nothing in her expression but sadness.

He passes Morrish Road. When they go over the bridge he looks at her again and sees her visibly shivering. He knows she's scared. He can feel it in the air. Matt begins feeling sympathy for her now and pulls over again. He looks into her black eyes and sees them slowly changing from black to sky blue. He asks her two questions. The first: "Do you promise to stop being violent and jealous?" She nods her head up and down. "Will you stop scaring away everybody that comes near me?" This time she doesn't nod.

A pained expression forms on her pretty face as she clearly strains. Her lips quiver mildly then an almost angelic voice says, "Yes. I promise."

He calls Caroline again and against his better judgment tells her he changed his mind and is going to give her a second chance.

Caroline begins pleading with Matt. "No! You can't, it's a trick. Don't trust her. She isn't your friend. You need to get here now!"

"If I need you, I'll call." Matt says.

"You won't be able to."

"Sorry to have wasted your time. Thanks anyways." He hangs up on her. He turns the car around and pulls away. He looks at the woman again and sees her smiling. As he passes Morrish road he feels her hand envelop his own. He is shocked as the woman unexpectedly straddles him. Matt feels cold lips press against his, her tongue enters his mouth. He knows this is wrong. He pushes her away. Nearing Elms Road he removes his foot from the accelerator and presses the brake. The car begins to slow.

She kisses him again, this time more forcefully. He tries to push her away but can't this time. He struggles for a second then gives up and lets her do what she pleases. It feels so good he now doesn't want her to stop. Her hand gently caresses his face. Her left hand begins rubbing his chest. She no longer feels cold against him. The car gets closer to the stop sign when she breaks the kiss and whispers three words to him. He says them back, then presses his lips back to hers as the car stops. He is intoxicated by her.

Out of nowhere the gas pedal is pushed to the floor by an invisible weight. As the car speeds from the stop sign she pulls her lips away, smiles and stares into his open eyes; he looks at peace. At this exact moment the small car is struck on the driver's side by a large truck.

Craig and Janice sit on their couch watching the newest episode of "The Walking Dead," getting ready to roll a joint and call it a night when they hear, in this order, tires screeching, a loud collision followed by crunching metal. The sounds are enough to make both of them jump up and rush to look out the front window. They quickly put their shoes on. Craig is the first through the front door, Janice hot on his heels, her phone held tightly in her hand.

The sight that lay before them unnerved them both. The driver of the truck crawls from the cab, his right hand holding his head with a river of steady flowing blood running between his fingers. The car looks as if it had just been in the grasp of a car crusher at the local junkyard. They get to the car, panting out of breath, and peer in through the gaping hole that was, up until less than five minutes ago, covered with glass. All they can make out is Matt's mangled, lifeless corpse with a smile on his face. They both think it quite odd that a corpse could have a smile.

Janice talks to the 911 operator, explaining what she saw in broken sentences. When she starts crying into the phone and can't get herself together, Craig takes it from her.

She looks away from the wreckage and two strangers catch her eye. Janice sees a man and a woman stepping into the woods that abutts their property and the road. They stop, turned around and stare at the totaled car. The man begins walking back towards the scene of the accident but is halted by the woman gently placing a hand on his shoulder. She says something to him but Janice can't tell what was said. Janice gets Craig's attention but he can't see anything.

When the first responders arrive, she tells them, "I seen a man and a woman I ain't never seen before going into our woods." When asked what the couple looked like, she answers, "The lady had long blonde hair, a ripped up dress, and was skinny." She pauses. "The man kinda looked like him." She points at the car. "She was smiling, but the guy looked really confused."

After she is shown a picture of Matt, she says that maybe it was his brother. Until she discovers that out of the other few witnesses, she was the only one to have seen them. Later, Craig would try to convince her that either her eyes were playing tricks on her, or that maybe it was a young couple trying to sneak off somewhere private. She knows in her heart that they were in the car. This was the point in Janice's life that she started believing in ghosts.

K.T. Lippert
My Summer Vacation

People are impressed when they learn that I did my first bank robbery (of many) at the age of 14, although it seems a grandiose to refer to that escapade as a bank robbery. The world is full of dreamers who think of ideas just like mine, but never act on them. I'm more of a doer.

During this time, Aunt Jane's Pickles was a major employer of high school kids in the area. They paid 60 cents a bucket for picking cucumbers. In reality, that was a pretty decent wage. If you were there to make money, you could go down a row picking with both hands, and fill a bucket in no time. It adds up quickly. When I took off on my Stingray that Saturday morning, I told Mom I was off to meet the truck that picked up workers at the grain elevators for a day of pickle picking.

Instead, I rode down to the park, stashed my bike, and retrieved the paraphernalia for my morning's work from my back pack. I had one of my sister's old wigs, which had long ago been relegated to the kid's room for Halloween dress up and what have you. I tucked in my t-shirt and pulled on a grossly oversized sweatshirt. My ensemble was completed with this ridiculous hat that was very in with 12-year-old girls that summer—a kind of sailor hat that pulled down over the eyes and had a strip of tinted vinyl in front that acted as sunglasses. I have no doubt that I looked very much like a 12-year-old girl as I strolled into the bank with that hat on over my blonde wig and my baggie sweatshirt.

I didn't hesitate—once through the door, I headed straight to an untended teller's window, and made a quick hop up onto the counter. I leaned over and started scooping up handfulls of cash from the drawer and stuffing them down the front of my shirt. Several of the bank patrons were looking at me with perplexed expressions, like they just couldn't quite comprehend what they were seeing. I kept at it until I was down to grabbing quarters and dimes. Finally a man in a suit came out of one of the offices and shouted, "Hey!" I hopped down and took off running—out the door, through the parking lot, across the firehouse lawn, through the cemetery, into the park and back to my bike. Nobody followed me. Within seconds, the wig and hat were shoved down into a trash can, the money was transferred to my backpack along with the sweatshirt, and I was pedaling back downtown in a leisurely fashion.

The scene around the bank was absolute chaos. Some Barney Fife deputy was outside the front door with his pistol in a two-handed grip, looking around wide-eyed. Both of the county cars were there, lights flashing, and a state police car was zooming in from the post just north of town, siren screaming and lights flashing. The crowd gathering outside was trembling with excitement. Rumors were already circulating about armed men in masks holding hostages and all manner of drama. I watched the show for a while and then moseyed on home.

I had picked this particular Saturday because the whole fam was scheduled to be off at some big-deal church function for the day and I would have the house to myself. (Had it not been for Aunt Jane's Pickles, I would have been forced to endure this affair, but—as important as it is to nurture the immortal soul—an honest day's labor for a fair wage is a sacred thing in itself, which provided the escape clause I needed. Thank you, Aunt Jane.)

Safely hidden away in my bedroom, I dumped my haul on a blanket on the floor. I had never seen so much money in my life. I counted it three times and ended up with hugely different totals each time. Ultimately, I just concentrated on making little piles of $100 each. These I double and triple checked. The quarters and dimes were built into stacks of $2 each. Using this approach, along with a paper and pencil, I eventually concluded that I had scored $1,647.85. One thousand, six hundred and forty seven American dollars, with an eighty five cent kicker. I was pretty sure that was most of the money in the whole, wide world.

My next question was, "Now what?" It's not like my family was so prosperous, or unaware of my doings, that I could just start accumulating shiny new possessions without notice. Strange as it may seem, the money wasn't really my motivation, and I hadn't given it a lot of thought. The doing of it was the point. The money itself was more a really swell fringe benefit.

One thing I knew I wanted was to get laid. In the big city, a guy with a pocket full of cash could have accomplished that goal in relatively short order. In my circumstance, though, it was a challenge. I set my sights on my best friend Dibs' sister Rita.

Dibs and his mom were working at the pickle station that summer—Dibs as a picker, his mom in the office. They dropped the younger sister off somewhere on the way and picked her up again after work. Rita stayed home, did the housework, and had dinner started when they came through the door. An ideal arrangement for my purposes.

The morning after my big score I took off—ostensibly to pick pickles—and did a little shopping. I went into several different stores making small purchases at each, accumulating the fixings for a truly outstanding pizza, and a six pack of RC Cola. Each store I went into, people were buzzing about the big robbery. Without exception, everything I heard was grossly inaccurate. I gave a high school kid two bucks to run me out to Dibs' house and pretended to be surprised when I asked for Dibs and Rita said that he was working. I told her I was trying to hide from my mom for the day and she invited me in.

Don't misunderstand. My mother is an exquisite human being. That's the problem. When your family is Evangelical, your mom is Aunt Bea, and everything is so freaking wholesome, sometimes you need to break out. Dibs' Mom was cool. She used to work in a bar, she let him have Playboys and everything. Their house was not utterly immaculate and everything was not in its assigned place at all times. There were usually dishes in the sink. It was comfortable. They felt sorry for me, and I was always welcome there.

I had known Rita literally all my life and regarded her as a kid sister, but something interesting had developed since last summer and I was beginning to see her in a whole different light. Rita was a little chubby, although she had become delightfully curvaceous. She had kind of a scratchy voice, and kinky hair and she laughed too loud. At the same time, she was cute and funny and I really liked hanging out with her.

That first day I helped her with the house work, we fixed pizza and just sort of lounged around for the afternoon. It was cozy. I could tell that she enjoyed it too, so I ventured to suggest we do it again tomorrow. She thought that was a splendid idea.

This quickly became our routine, and as the days went by, our meals became more and more elaborate. It was into the third week before we did the deed.

I have to admit, the first go-round was pretty amateurish, and not so gratifying for either of us. When it was over we looked at each other and both burst out laughing. I'll say this for us, though: neither of us were quitters. We hung in there and over a period of time, I think we got pretty good at it.

Throughout this time, nobody knew our secret. It was assumed that I was out picking pickles, and no one suspected that Rita didn't spend her days alone. At the end of every week I would flash some money around at home and humbly accept the praise I received for my outstanding work ethic. I hung out with Dibs some evenings and on weekends, like always. I'd see Rita and we'd kid around like we always had. Nobody suspected a thing.

It was great, but all good things must come to an end. What was cool about us is that we didn't have that clingy, desperate, can't-live-without-your-touch thing going on. We both knew that when it was over, it was over; we didn't even try to figure out a way to keep it going. The summer came to an end, and with it our foray into domestic bliss.

Our last day together, I confessed that when I showed up there that first day, my intentions, as they say, were not honourable. "Gee," she deadpanned, "I hadn't guessed." On my way out the door, I handed her a $100 bill, which she calmly accepted with a quiet "Thanks," folded into quarters, and slid into her back pocket. Throughout the summer I had brought her little gifts, small things that wouldn't raise any eyebrows—a couple different record albums, a few little trinkets I knew she'd enjoy—which she accepted gracefully. She never questioned how I financed the lavish meals or any of the rest of it. I told her, "It is important nobody know where that came from."

"I know where it came from," she said. From the expression in her eyes, I knew that she somehow did. "Don't worry, I'll never tell." After a long pause, I kissed her on the forehead, turned, and left.

Life took us down separate paths after that and other things filled the space she and Dibs had occupied. A few years later he was killed in Viet Nam, and I have never seen Rita since.

She ended up marrying a very square guy with an office job. She is doing the suburban soccer mom thing now and is apparently pretty content. True to her word, she never told, not even after the bank offered a substantial reward for information.

During the summer of 1967, I became a millionaire, ate a lot of good food, and learned some important life lessons I didn't even realize until much later. I think of Rita often, and every time the thought causes a little twinge in my heart. I think of her as my first love and the classiest chick I ever knew.

David Michael Martin
Renoir Goes to Market

Paris, 1896, the first Sunday of spring, and the sun is shining in the midday sky. A white-topped, grey-bottomed rogue cloud, a dirty iceberg in a sea of blue, drifts across the city, dropping a feathery mist that lays on my sleeves like dust rather than soaking into the cotton fibers. Some of the people walking beside me groan, disappointed. The light drizzle floats down onto the boulevard, but now, perversely, it evaporates before hitting the ground. The spitting stops, and a few of the optimists in the crowd pause and shake fine droplets from their parasols. I smile to myself as they gaze up at the mischievous cloud. A timid breeze ruffles coattails and dresses in reply, a hint that we might receive another brief misting soon.

Shifting motion in the crowd catches my notice. At first I assume that it is the bourgeois lady wearing a fine cotton dress who piques my interest, but she is only glancing down at a little girl, smiling. The girl leans against the woman's side, her mother of course, fidgeting: a filly stamping her hooves. A blossoming young woman, apparently an older sister, rests a firm hand on the girl's upper arm, bridling her impatience.

The girl holds onto an annealed metal hoop and a strip of wood, a toy, unwilling to chance losing it in the crowded street. I have little doubt that she is on her way to the park, too. There she can chase after the metal hoop to her heart's content, pushing and prodding it with the stick while running alongside after it—her dress, lace, and bonnet rippling in the turbulence of her galloping.

She turns her head, her eyes narrowing in apparent mistrust.

At me, I wonder? No. I follow her gaze, searching for what was provoking the little princess's enmity.

Ahead of us, a plain, young, determined proletarian woman in a well-worn but clean black wool dress steps out of the wooded park in the boulevard's medial strip. She is moving against the crowd toward us. A market basket hangs from her forearm. The angle of her arm and the way the basket swings against her hip tells me that it is empty.

I watch the woman step between the little girl and me. The resigned grimace on her face reminds me that not for everyone today is a Sunday walk to a place of rest and play.

"Excuse me, Mademoiselle," I call out. "Why are you in such a hurry? The mist has stopped and your dress will soon dry in the warm sun."

"I beg your pardon, Monsieur, but I cannot tarry," she gasps.

"But why not?" I ask. "The day is young."

"Forgive me, Monsieur, but I must make my way through the crowds to Pierre's Market on the Rue de Baton. It is a long way to go and time is short."

"But if I may say so, Mademoiselle, Jean-Jacques' Market is only a short walk back the way you came."

"Oui, Monsieur. I know. I just came from there. Jean-Jacques has nothing that I can afford to buy today."

"But you might not reach Pierre's Market before he too sells out his dregs of the day. Here now, take these four centimes and go back to Jean-Jacques' to buy what you need. . . "

The young woman stops and whirls on me.

"Non! Monsieur! I am a good Christian woman. I am no beggar. Nor do I do the dance of the evening!"

"I only offer in the name of true Christian charity, Mademoiselle. I mean no insult."

"And I thank you for your charity, Monsieur," she stammers, "but if I had need of charity, I would be even now on my way to the friars for soup and bread. Even I give a centime in the offering for the poor at mass."

My surprise must be showing, for her stern features soften.

"Do you see all these people milling around us, Monsieur? They are going about their lives in an orderly fashion. I too have my business to be about. I am poor, but I am not destitute. The problem with charity is that it is neither constant nor does it promote self-sufficiency. At least in public I have my dignity and my pride. If you feel the need to give to charity, Monsieur, then please give your money to the friars and help those who truly have need of it."

The woman pauses, draws a deep breath, gazes down the boulevard, and sighs. Shifting the empty market basket back into the crook of her arm, she bids me a parting sentiment.

"Thank you again for your kindness, Monsieur."

Justin Monson
The Man at the Corner Table

I had driven in the rain to the apartment we once shared. She said, Stephen I'm just happy we can be civil about this. Dr. Taylor always tells me, There's something to be said about two adults accepting that the time has come for them to find happiness on their own. —Yes, I said, I remember her saying that in those last sessions. She placed the last cardboard box of my possessions into my hands and leaned against the front door, hands on her hips, and I looked inside the half-empty box. She could have just thrown the stuff away. Five picture frames; my broken espresso machine; three of my dress shirts she had commandeered in the early days of our marriage and had not touched since the Madrid situation; and a stack of ballet and play programs that we had saved over the years, stretching back to our first date. The program at the top of the rubber-banded stack was from last September's showing of A Human Being Died That Night. Not often can a man plot the precise coordinates of his marriage unraveling, but I've always had a keen eye for tipping points. When the protagonist of the production finally began to understand the psyche of the notorious criminal she has been interviewing, she walked off stage, leaving the man to sit in the concrete solitude he had always longed for but feared. Right there in Section A, Row 1, Seat 12, my wife began to cry. A month later she left me a note on the kitchen counter when she left for work. I read the long-handed cursive aloud: I'll say it first since I know you won't. We are broken. We need a divorce. I'm sorry for whatever I've done. —Sophie Standing in the hallway with my box of remnants I said, Sophie, you know we could —She said, I don't want to sound rude, but I have an appointment with Dr. Taylor at seven —Oh. Yes, I said, I have to get going myself. One of my students wanted to meet about her thesis paper. —Oh, well I'm sorry I've kept you. I know how important your students are. — Soph, it's not like —It's okay, Stephen. You don't have to defend yourself anymore. I've got to get ready. Give Rocky a treat for me? She opened the front door. All right, I said. —All right, she said. She closed the door behind me and I walked to my car as fast as I could. While in grad school, before I met Sophie, I always found the older men who sat alone drinking coffee in cafés to be quite pathetic. I thought, How can a man resign himself to that sort of existence while the world is so ripe for the picking? Clichés become so easily accepted at twenty-four and young men always feel their vitality will never dissolve. Now it is Friday evening in early June and I am sitting at a corner table in the food co-op a block from my rented flat; though to be fair, the café area is actually relatively open, thus the corner table is surrounded by open space and florescent lighting. The half-empty cardboard box still sits in the trunk of my car. It has been three days. I am rotating a cup of scalding microwaved coffee in tight circles between my fingers and watching the young woman three tables away from me eating a light dinner—maybe a snack, who knows these days?—and the little boy who is pouting about tofu or something-or-other, sitting in a cart that he clearly outgrew a few years ago. The boy's mother is reading a magazine while the boy looks to be talking to himself and wiping tears from his cheeks with the tops of his wrists. This coffee tastes pitiful. I am on the cusp of 48. I've always been well-built. My age has never bothered me, nor has it ever seemed to be a factor in how younger men treated me. That is, until 10 minutes ago when the young gentleman behind the coffee counter spoke to me as if I lack understanding of basic thermodynamics. After putting just a drip, just a drip, of hazelnut creamer into my dark roast, it occurred to me that my coffee was barely room temperature. What then does this lofty-looking barista say to me upon hearing my grievance? Well, sir, I think when you put in cold creamer it cools off. Sophie used to tell me that I put on airs when I am offended, that I am far too easy-going to be truly upset that my steak was cooked rare when I clearly asked for it to be medium, or that the male nurses she worked with kept asking her out to dinner. She would say, sweetheart, please stop, we both know you're not truly upset. Then she would clasp my hand and run her thumb over the divots between my knuckles. After accusing the barista of patronizing and talking down to me, my knuckles felt bare. The mother of the tofu-child has noticed me staring at her little boy. He has been moaning for some time now about his predicament, crying and telling his mother he is going to eat himself. He has taken to nibbling at his arms and yelling through his sobs, nom nom nom see Mom? I taste good but the tofu scares me! The boy's mother closes her magazine, looks at me and asks me, is there something I can help you with sir? I am put off by the way she says sir. That word affects me in ways I cannot understand. Are we not two travelers, passing one another in transit? Oh, no not at all, I say, I'm sorry I must have been lost in thought. Cute kid. —Looking at the boy and messing his hair she says, yes, my little monster. —Quite an eccentric one —Oh yes, I suppose he gets it from his father, she says. Don't they all? I say in jest. My joke has made her uncomfortable and her lips are pursed now. She says, yes, I suppose so, and returns to her magazine. I look at the face of my cell phone and notice my features reflecting on its surface. The bags under my eyes take up more real estate than they once did. They look stuffed with middle age. I feel ridiculous. Not often do I allow myself to indulge in this brand of self-pity. Men are not supposed to be this way, unhappy while alone. Solitude should always be a man's great desire, my father used to say as we fished off the shores of the sound. When I got married I asked him why he never seemed bothered when we drove home without fish. He put his hands on my shoulders and said, we don't go out there to bring back fish, son. When my father passed away I placed both of our fishing rods in his coffin with him. I suddenly remember that I no longer have sentimental commitments, if I ever truly conformed to such things. I glance once more at the bags under my eyes, then liven my phone. Scrolling past names in my contacts, I stop at Renata Choi. She's witty and opposed to conventional monogamy and she has "Free Spirit" tattooed in tiny cursive on her forearm. I text her: Thinking about dessert at Cousteau's. Care to join? Drinks after? The young woman eating a light dinner three tables away writes in short strokes into a leather-bound notebook in between bites of salad. She chews politely and I begin to wonder what she writes about. No, whom she writes about. All literature at its core is about a single human being. I fantasize she is writing about me, about the dashing man sitting at the corner table somehow independent of the troubles that plague most men, until she notices me looking at her. I pretend that I am looking behind her, shifting in my chair to give my act a look of authenticity. I could have been a method actor. My phone lights up with a text from Renata Choi and I read: So cute that you thought of me! I'd love to but I have a dinner engagement tonight. Late brunch tomorrow? My father used to sit me down and tell me, Stevie, your mother is very busy this weekend so she can't come pick you up but she wanted me to tell you that she loves you very much. Eventually my time spent with her became exclusive to important holidays. For a while I think of texting Sophie but decide it not a fruitful idea. The neuroses of that span of my life are no longer my cross to bear. Still, I am gazing into the light of my phone, Sophie's name stuck on the screen. My coffee has grown cold. What is that quote my students seemed to be so distracted with last week? "Man is born free, but is everywhere in chains?" Yes. That is the one. I gulp down the last of my cold coffee. Now what to do? I think of asking the woman reading her magazine if she would like to join me for dessert at Cousteau's. I'm sure her son would like a change of scenery. No, best not to get involved with whatever mother-son bonding they are aiming for. Maybe he doesn't see her often. Maybe I could strike up a conversation with the young woman, who is now pecking away at her laptop with an absorbed look to her that I find admirable. I could offer to take a look at her writing and we could share lush words until the barista begins to close the café area and edge us out. We could exchange numbers and agree to meet up next Friday to discuss culture and literature and the importance of postmodern art, though somewhere with a bit more class. I stand out of my chair with that curious dignity one feels when he has flushed away all indecisiveness. I voyage the first step toward the young woman, who has just elegantly folded her legs into full-lotus and now reminds me of the origami cranes I made for girls when I was in third grade. I'm looking at her expecting her to notice and make eye contact. Why isn't she noticing me? Again she's beginning to lay short strokes in her leather-bound notebook with a brilliant green pen. For fear that my measured strides should appear too measured, I look down at my watch as I walk past the girl in full-lotus and mutter, hmm I thought it was much later. Standing at the coffee counter I read the entire menu 10 times over. After seriously considering five flavors of scones, I purchase another cup of dark roast. I skip the hazelnut creamer. Turning back to my corner table I notice a void. The girl in full-lotus has left. Walking to my corner table I casually look around. Maybe she needed to stretch her legs. Again I feel ridiculous for hoping that things would really pan out differently from what is expected. The lights in this area are far too bright, as if at once we are all about to be interrogated. The woman is still reading her magazine, though now the little boy is giving an evil stare to his tofu plate, his brow turned down and his cheeks flushed. I sit for a while, nursing my coffee. Eventually, the little boy digs into his tofu with a plastic sample spoon and he seems to thoroughly enjoy the texture because with each successive bite he smacks his lips and smiles and giggles. Such a nice little loop of happiness. Tofu eaten he says, Mom. Mom mom mom mom. Mom, I finished. I like tofu now! Look, he says, stretching his arm to wave the empty plate in front of her nose. He tosses the plate on to the table from his seat in the cart and wipes his hands on the front of his shirt, which is white with an electric-blue monochrome image of Albert Einstein with a frazzled mane printed on the front. The bottom of the image reads: "E=MC^{haired}." If I had a son I think I'd buy him this shirt. The boy's mother says to him, that's good Tyson, good job, then messes his hair and begins to clear the table of her magazine and chai tea, her son's empty plate. He asks, can I have some more, Mom? I like tofu now. —No honey that's enough, she says, you should have started liking it earlier. Now we have to take you to Dad's house. —But I don't wanna go to Dad's. I want more tofu, Mom. I like it now! The little boy grabs fists of his hair in his hands as he pleads with his mother. My leg is shaking under the table and my mouth is dry, tense. She says, I'm sorry honey, I'm sorry, then looks around in the sad, nervous manner people sometimes betray. Except for the barista, I am the only other person in the café area. My phone slips around in my clenched hand. What is happening to me? Dammit, how long have I been squeezing it like this? I feel as if I am suffocating in my own skin. I've got to get out of here. Outside, the crisp air calms me a bit. I amble west on Fourth Avenue, for what reason I do not know, but it feels right. I walk for a while, passing young couples and homeless people pushing their carts. I give a few dollars to a man who is missing his left eye. How lonely a homeless person must feel. Where will this man with one eye go after there are no pedestrians to hand him folded up dollars? Then I am standing on the corner of Fourth Avenue and Maple, across the street from Cousteau's. Through the restaurant's bay window I see Sophie sitting alone in the booth we have shared on so many nights. Her elbow rests on the table and her cheek is pressed against her palm. She's looking down at her phone with a defeated look. the people walking past me are making an exaggerated point of saying excuse me as they walk around me. This makes sense, I suppose, since I'm standing in the middle of a busy sidewalk. I sit on a nearby stone bench where I still have an open view of Cousteau's bay window and the world unfolding inside. After 10 minutes of typing then subsequently deleting texts to my wife, I opt for a simple message: *I miss you.* I'm pressing send. From across the street I watch Sophie read my message, set her phone down and take a long drink of her wine. Then she presses her hands together and looks up as if saying a prayer before anyone notices. She used to perform this minute supplication whenever she was scared of something. Though she'll never admit it, every time we flew she whispered her abbreviated prayer before takeoff. Every time. And every time I asked her if she was all right she would pat my arm and say, of course sweetheart, why do you ask? Sophie cradles her phone in her lap for a few minutes and then I receive her reply: *I miss you too, Stephen. This is harder for me than you know, admitting that to you.* How many times can this situation replay itself in a relationship, this cat-and-mouse game of drinking liquids alone in establishments and drafting short messages over long deliberations? I write to her: *I want to see you. Why don't we meet at Cousteau's and talk? No fighting, just conversation and laughter.* I'm pressing send. A young couple sharing a Styrofoam bowl of frozen yogurt sits down next to me. I can see their reckless infatuation with one another by the way they take purposeful little bites and pass the spoon back and forth in blissful silence. A language for two binds any couple together in ways they struggle to explain but everyone around them immediately becomes aware of. Trying to explain the patterns woven by such a language, if you are one of the two who speak it, is a moonshot at best. Sophie replies: *I'd like that. I'll call ahead and have them save our table. Twenty minutes?* I laugh outwardly, loud enough to startle the couple next to me. I say, excuse me, sorry about that. A friend just sent me a very funny YouTube video. One of the young women smiles and says, by all means. Don't excuse yourself, laughter's a gift. What's the video of? I say, oh n-nothing, just a bit of an inside joke. The other young woman nods her head knowingly and they continue sharing their frozen yogurt. I send my reply: *See you soon.* I look to Sophie through the window across the street. She is speaking to the waiter, pointing at the seat across from her. The waiter takes her wine glass then brings back two cups of ice-water and a dessert menu. Sophie takes off her glasses and rubs the bridge of her nose with her index fingers. She runs her fingers backwards through her hair. I sit on the stone bench for 15 minutes, watching the city light refract and float away into the naked sky. Tomorrow, I'll buy a new fishing rod. It's been much too long. I stand and turn to the young couple. I say, Always remember your language. They must have not heard me, or they don't realize I am speaking to them, because they aren't acknowledging me whatsoever. They are only passing the spoon back-and-forth, taking hopeful little bites as if nothing else matters.

Corey Joseph Montague
The Legend of Funky Zero

I live in New York City. I work for a major brokerage house on Wall Street. Please allow me to inconvenience you for a spell by telling you about a bonafide idiotic associate of mine. His name is Zero Larizzio. At 36, he is the sort of chump in passing you'd look at in awe more than thrice. Zero is a second-generation Italian. But he eats Romanian, Greek, French, Hindu, and Soul Food. Anything except Italian foods. And he can tell you the precise seasoning ingredients in every morsel of every bite in any culinary dish he tastes. He said to me:

"I only eat caviar from the Caspian Sea."

"I only eat mine out of neighborhood supermarket tins."

"Hummm, an uneducated palate."

"Uh huh, you're correct again as usual," I agreed just to placate him, because he is the know-it-all type.

To let him tell it, he knows more about cheese than Velveeta. This guy is an almanac, a clearinghouse of frivolous information. He once claimed he knew the exact amount of sesame seeds McDonald's puts on their Big Mac buns sold worldwide for the last 29 years within a margin of error of five seeds. And the time it took for an obese man to make a bowel movement after consuming 10 pounds of pasta. He'd make ludicrous claims like his ancestors invented adultery, daylight saving time, and the hairbrush. Now get this, he claimed he knows how many foul balls were hit in Yankee Stadium from 1945 to 2015, and how many Yankee fans farted in the stadium since 1962. Oh this guy is a bedroom-variety super dildo. But what constantly got me was he seemed so damn convincing. Straight face and all. The guy talked to associates like he actually knew what he was talking about. He also convinced me. If anyone ever doubted him, he'd offer his ever-present laptop for proof. He'd say:

"If you don't believe me, look it up."

"Now what site would I visit to research some frivolous drug like that?"

"Gaggle it."

I thought he'd said Google it. He had a website called, FrivolousInfo.com. But at the time I didn't know that was his personal webpage. Oh this guy was a real penitentiary cell door. Once you got inside, he wasn't hardly going to let you go unless he unlocked the fucking door! As for sexual experience, all he knew about was his right hand. A real life masturbation artist. When it came to women, Zero was a funky zero. He couldn't make a starving woman come for a dinner bell—until he came up with another one of his frivolous concoctions. This time he boasted a love potion—but I digress. I'll explain that later.

No, on second thought, I won't.

"A woman is why Cain killed Abel," Zero said.

"What?! Are you nuts? Or are you simply stark raving mad? Why do you suggest that?" I inquired.

"Back in 45 B.C., there were only four Jews on earth. Three males and one female. So sayeth the bible. Now reverse roles. Wouldn't you be horny as hell if there was only one man in the world and he just so happened to be your father? And you had to take turns screwing him with your mother and sister watching. Your aggressive personality suggests your mother and sister had to go!"

"My God, you're sick!" I said.

"I didn't kill Abel," he smugly replied. "Nor did I pan the bible. That's God's story. He can tell it any time he wants to." I was ashamed to admit he made sense. One time I told him I wasn't fond of taking prescription medications for stomach aches (irritable bowel syndrome), so he gave me a home remedy of vinegar, baking soda, and warm water. I took the cure, and bon voyage went my bellyache. But hello, Roman numeral flatulence. And eight days later my stool was still baby-food soft.

Then there was the time he gave me a cure for my menstrual bloating. I was actually dumb enough to listen—but I digress. I'll get back to that one later. No, perhaps not. It's far too embarrassing. Zero's got this scientific theory of the world's land mass shrinking. As if he were some type of earth wheel geologist roaming the globe collecting trivial dates. He said by the year 145,000,000 A.D. the whole world would be the size of Rhode Island. Like anyone would be alive to give a damn!

Zero spoke with such great authority on all things frivolous and mundane. The University of Magicians, Clowns, and Circus Critics should've given him a Master's degree in Convincing Bullshit! I mean this guy studied the dictionary like peeping toms study open windows. Everywhere he went, he carried a laptop and a hardcover Webster's dictionary. I was briefly intrigued by this guy. So one day at work I caught myself setting him up. I asked Zero if he knew how to spell "prognosticate" (I already had the correct spelling written in my palm). No problem, this guy rattled it off. I just wanted to see if he was on the level. I was amazed. This guy pretended to be a genius on so much frivolous garbage it was astounding. I actually fell all the way up to my nose into his pseudo-psychodramatic landfills.

Then there was the time I went up to his Upper East Side apartment to retrieve an important client's portfolio. While there he explained an important experiment with three different species of cockroaches: a big one, a bigger one, and an enormous one with wings. He claimed he needed their DNA to concoct a weight loss serum. He said he was working on a cure for morbid obesity. Now that to me wasn't too bizarre. Since this guy was as fat as the lightest contestant on TLC's *My 600-lb Life*. About three months later at lunch he stood in front of everyone with a digital scale. He weighed himself, 460 pounds.

About two weeks after that, what do you know? Ol' Zero came back to work weighing a remarkable 170 pounds soaking wet. This guy had the audacity to be handsome, and as thin as a Ritz Cracker held up sideways. No one could believe it. But we had to. It was a miracle! This guy had every overweight and bulimic girl in our office eating out of the palm of his manicured hand. He had so much office sex he walked around bowlegged. A few of those ladies I liked and respected. A number of the more handsome men in the office were, of course, jealous. But anyway all 26 ladies in our office worshipped him. For five days Zero was the rock star of Wall Street.

However, over the weekend he shoots back up to 460 pounds. Needless to say he was still the main attraction. He explained his weight gain. There were some minor inconsistencies in the formula. But he was working on a correction. He quickly gave us a confusing bout of Chemistry 101. So before he got too deep, I faded back to my cubicle, still spellbound. Again this guy takes us back on another one of his many mindfucks. Next he says, he invented a cure for incarceration. By gene splicing. He said when a zygote is inside a mother's womb, a prenatal microsurgeon could go in and extract DNA strands from the fetus, then take samples for possible criminal tendencies against other criminals in the World DNA Database. If the genes' test results were positive, then removal of the gene is warranted, therefore eliminating a need for people to commit crimes. The end result: termination of prisons and/or incarceration.

Now I got to thinking about the socioeconomic domino aftereffect of no crime. I said, what about prison guard's livelihoods, police, judges, lawyers, prosecutors, jailers, halfway houses, parole, and probations officers all of them would be unemployed. Not to mention the industries that thrive directly and indirectly off prison commerce: businesses in rural areas, like gas stations, motels, hotels and restaurants. All would go out of business with the loss of crime, because prisoners' family members would stop spending in rural economies. For without crime it would wreak havoc on the world economies. Wall Street stock markets would become capricious because of the loss of investment capital in privatized prison stocks. In essence, America desperately needed crime in order to support its shrinking middle classes.

"So, give them the criminal gene," Zero supplied.

"But fool that would still leave criminals."

"Not really, because those guys on Wall Street can afford attorneys."

Footnote:

P.S.: Zero never lost weight. That fat freak is an identical twin. But he did manage to trick a lot of female associates out of sex, and investment capital (I had relations with him also, and paid him to do it. I guess because at the time it was the most fashionable thing to do.) Eventually he manipulated his way to a supervisory position. That "harasshole" is now my boss. I paid for this message to self-destruct. But I doubt it will.

Sincerely yours,
Disgruntled Anonymous Associate

Steven L. Montez
Believe

I awoke this morning to the memory of a dream about tiny footprints and snow, and walls that fell long ago when I believed that the world was bigger than it is. I awoke this morning with a perspicuous image of a smile I hadn't seen in six long years on a face whose clarity I believed would only fade. I woke this morning to hear once upon a time knocking helter-skelter at the doorstep of here and now—and for a second I believed it might be answered by tomorrow. I awoke this morning contemplating the frailty and mystery of belief. Wondering if I had ever truly believed anything in my life, and if so, if it ever made a bit of difference. If it was wise. If it was pointless. If it was folly. If it was prudent. If it was sane. If it was possible.

As the day progressed I found myself immersed in the catharsis of an accidental inventory of what I believe. And the truth is that it wasn't such a bad place to linger for a while. The lights were bright in the darkness. The shelter shadowed against the abyss of what we know to be unknown. Sanctuary of this sort is strong. Believing, after all, is far more comforting that wondering, more peaceful than doubting, and too often less grievous than knowing. At least that's what I believe.

I believe in dirt roads and the duality of destiny, the scent of an old lilac bush that knew no barrier at my bedroom window, the stories and names and tears in the soil of a mountain mile, choices that require effort to make *and* to fulfill, the treacherous space between vanity and self-respect, and the wildness of letting it be. I believe in dry flies and dry humor, the last drop of a downpour and the first snowflake of winter, the sweet siren-song of waterfalls and the long ambiguous silence of Cooney's tomb and Jennie's grave, and the last few moments before daybreak. I believe in living long enough to have a story to tell, and dying well enough to leave a little mystery. I believe in a world where people aren't judged solely on the worst thing they have ever done, in a truth that is not simply what those in power deem it to be, and in doing what we have to do in order to do what we gotta do. I believe in flesh, fury, flame, an existence known viscerally, a permanence that is greater than married or broken or dead, and the crucial difference that often lives between facts and truth. I believe in virtue, but no more than in evil. I believe in tomorrow, but a little less than in yesterday. I believe in heaven, but also the hell along the winding road that leads to its gate.

I believe that we all have more than one true love, and that still many people never find it, and that we all must go to California at some point, no matter where or what our California is. I believe that jam tastes better than jelly, that fall is more spiritual than spring, that night is holier than day, that a man with no enemies is the greatest of warriors, that accidental meetings aren't, that it means very little without eye contact, and that ordinary is too boring, too cowardly, too fatally easy. I believe that water can be much thicker than blood, that first times are more memorable even though last times are more important, that Alex was right to cross the Teklanika, that every single human being in the world is a musician, that only the guilty sleep well at night, that breasts are the perfect drug, and that the answer to life might just be 42 after all. I believe that power comes from the knowledge we possess, but strength comes from how we use that knowledge, that walls are at their strongest after they fall, that the difference between saying it and singing it is whether or not you live it, and that if I am able to fish one more time I will catch a mermaid with sea-green eyes.

I believe in haunted houses and afterglow, show & tell and thunder, circles I have stood in, and the ripples on Tearwater Pond. I believe in Judgment Day—and it usually arrives long before we die. I believe in the euphoria of wild enchantment and the harmony of right names spoken with trembling bravery, ketchup on macaroni & cheese and unexpected kindness, the poetry of paradox, and the health properties found in rainbow sherbet and black jelly beans. I believe in looking past what we believe we know, daily acts of personal rebellion and society outrage, the unplanned benefits of being crazy, kisses that have both history and future, buckets of salvation that arrive none too soon, and everyday altruism and grace. I believe in death with all possible dignity, the divine eccentricity that lies within each of us, the unwelcome incipience of truth and quietus, the lifelong battle between the skeletons in the closet and the monsters under the bed, and the ghost that stood on my back porch just long enough to say goodbye.

I believe that the next time around I will be skinnier and have more hair, that one day I will become a bird, that I was loved consummately at least once, that food is more nourishing when it is seasoned with good company, that with us forever are those things left unsaid, that we do not understand everything that we have accepted, that the purest form of support is that which was not asked for, that you can't throw yourself in front of beauty without getting some of it on you, and that the first place we go when we die is to the last place we truly loved. I believe that two people can accomplish anything together until one does something that can't be undone, that sometimes the only way to ease another's agony is to endure your own, and that the most honest thing a person can do is live unapologetically by his creed. I believe that even though love and fantasy are what we write about, sex and death are why we write, that the most amazing erotic encounter of my life is the one that's happening next, and that there is no higher religion than to gaze upon others with empathy and respect. I believe that rivers speak in riddles and metaphor—and if we are patient and lucky, we hear the words that matter. I believe that memories are stronger than mortality, that wisdom begins in wonder, that what we see is what we are, and that the most translucent color is deep, deep blue.

I believe in messed-up beds, anticipation that borders on frenzy, cursing with panache, the beauty of snakes and spiders, the fleeting dash of black and white dog fur that I still occasionally swear I can glimpse out of the corner of my eye, and dancing with the person who brought you. I believe in the infallible protection of homemade forts, whether they are constructed of wood and nail in a tree behind the house of your teens, or of old blankets in the darkest corner of your childhood home. I believe in pondering, dissecting, musing about good people's wicked acts and bad people's admirable ones, and the seemingly accidental nature of the amatory exploits of my life. I believe in the empowerment granted by necessity, the courage afforded by education, and the melody that arises from the concord union of self-effort and unmerited help. I believe in "what if?" and "maybe tomorrow," life before death, the rare haven and contentment of invisibility, hot cider and warm doughnuts, coda in a minor key, decarceration, the will of spawning salmon, Pay Attention moments, hillbilly scholars, the fidelity of fighting for hopeless causes, the fickle unpredictability of hatred, the heroism of humility, the honor of a rigid moral code, and mercy for my mother and my sister and my niece.

I believe that letting go is impossible—and unwise, that laughter is the second best medicine—right behind love, that there is no such thing as a clean kill, and that everything causes cancer. . . faith, family, freedom. . . hope. Everything. I believe that people rarely comprehend the enormity of even the simplest of promises while they are making them. Still, I believe that when they vow not to leave us, forsake us, forget us, hurt us, stop loving us that they mean it. . . in that moment. I believe that moments pass faster than miles, and miles pass faster than we expect them to, no matter how many times we take a particular route. I believe that the character of the people who admire or condemn us give us the truest reflection of who we are, that security is a superstition, that music is the only real miracle found in organized religion, and that people can do damn near anything and get away with it if they are attractive. I believe that nobody remains innocent very long, that not every loss screams for remembrance, and that to be great is to be vulnerable. . . and vice versa. I believe that even though we must die alone, we cannot live alone, and that how a person's life is spent affects mostly himself, but how it ends affects those to whom he is beloved. I believe that style is a poor substitute for substance, that you can only carry demons and angels around on your shoulders for so long before they tear you apart, that leaves simply let go more often than they wither and fall, and that the most important markings on any tombstone have little to do with birth or death, but instead, the mosaic of granite on which they are engraved.

I believe in dreams and nightmares, and the sliver of perspective that divides and defines them. I believe in the power of peace, the sagacity of Carlin and Clower, the view from Mount LeConte, and apologies that don't require prompting. I believe in scenic routes, blood-red sunsets, love big enough to be misunderstood by small minds, wrestling smart, grace notes that other people can't hear, a good left cross, and the evergold buried in the dirt underneath. I believe in Bigfoot, normal, and God equally. I believe in the symbiosis of fate and entropy, the strength of simplicity, the moment that the journey takes us, good girls, bad intentions, and the lucidity of gray. I believe in spinning round in circles, arms raised, eyes closed, smiling, crying. I believe in the epiphany of getting found when all you've known is lost, and the liberty of getting lost when the muck of life won't stop finding you. I believe in the universal, if sometimes muffled or incoherent, language of lust, the prepossessing pain that burns in my legs during a walk into the wild, the reflection and providence that coexist in pristine repose, and the waning, though still breathing, hope that I have done enough to secure a place in her memory. I believe in the lessons about living that dying teaches us, the lights that hover over Keeler Cemetery, the medicine found in the scent of burning leaves, much of what lies sleeping under the kudzu, the wrinkled photo in my pocket, returning to places we've never been, the terrible intimacy of ever-raw scars—especially the ones no one else can see, the privilege of reverence, a manner of living that shatters other people's assumptions, and suffering sublimely.

I believe that self-righteousness comes easily when it is other people's evil you are judging, that real friendship bends before it breaks, that there is no more desperate illusion than just enough love, that there is nothing sexier than dark makeup running down from teary uplifted eyes, that we are depicted by our worst moment only by those who have never had their own extraordinary moment, and that lemonade sipped from a Mason jar is better than the finest wine, but not quite as good as it is from a plastic cup at a child's lemonade stand. I believe that there are a hundred ways to embrace the earth, a thousand ways to show love, a million ways to pray, and that enlightenment lies at the confluence of the many twisting tributaries that flow through a person's life—by way of struggle as well as fortune, hedonism as well as austerity, faith as well as doubt. I believe that wounds do not heal properly by pretending that the injury never happened, that nobody truly knows when they are at their most beautiful, that willows weep for a reason, that the long day closes too early and without consent or compassion or malice or sympathy, that alive is a matter of perception, that we become immortal the second we come to know another like no one else has ever known them, and that there are killers and stars and fair ladies and gentlemanly dogs who know my name. Who will always know my name.

I awoke this morning to memory and mirror. I awoke this morning to mystery and the gentle ebb of maybe. I awoke this morning to the peal of yesterday's voices whispering secrets about things that I couldn't possibly know—unless I found a way to trust, to accept fully without understanding, to know the unprovable, to see and feel all that is brilliant behind an opaque cloud of a life lived urgently, torturously, defiantly, purely. . . exquisitely, and not quite over. I awoke this morning to belief. I believe, because I awoke this morning.

Bryan Palmer
The Building Code

I.

The decrepit buildings of Detroit whisper as I stride past, a fast jog really, you wouldn't want to linger about. They're houses of horrors, fun houses to some, sad memories to others, of the lost souls trapped inside forever more. To the homeless, these vacant dwellings are but a fleeting claim of salvation from the elements that kill: frostbitten digits, noses blackened by gangrene, or if they're lucky, pneumonia sets in from the deluge of water wrecking fragile cardboard homes, and they're stacked in hospitals like diseased cordwood.

The callous houses are eerily silent except to those who care to listen to the savage stories within. Graffiti speaks volumes to the hearing impaired, of the sets and crews who came before and may never have left, leaving charred, blackened shells to remain, stray dogs to roam the interiors, rabid and hungry for flesh. Blood-tipped needles pepper the rubbish-swelled floor, remnants of the heroin craze that grips those who crawl through the crumbling, poverty door.

Late at night, when the clouds shroud the moon and shadowy figures, you can hear the tortured howls and thumps of bodies being dumped: whores who have enraged their pimps, leaving black and blue marks, HIV infected, sides to hump.

I witness these untold abominations, behind closed blinds, stories rarely shared the political/tabloid masses. Shattered streetlights, and crimson-yellow stained mattresses lined up like a sleazy motel, garbage bag coffee tables, diapered doilies, and riven glass floors defy the chorus line of what's in store.

Bumpin' rides streaming rap music on 24s, vibrating bass, AK-47's blindly slicing any race, déjà vu.

II.

I don't move because I'm old, older than most, younger than some. Where would I go? To some infantile nursing home and have others tell me what to do? Here I can take my own pot shots, like Dirty Harry, but nowadays, more like Gran Torino. I've dragged my own bodies in and out of the cinder block cemeteries, with newspaper epitaphs and milk crate tombstones.

Each twilight is movie night: the OK Corral, Death Wish, Faces of Death, Crime Stoppers Matinee; don't hold your breath. Hundreds of dozens reside in these poor gated communities, where no one wants to get in and no one can get out. The barriers to destitution are portals to personal hells, either internal or external.

The dainty, yellow daffodils that filled ceramic flower boxes in the 60s withered into dusty fields where weeds don't dare grow lest they get shot for being on the wrong block, a glock full of shells littered after the last one tried to run the gauntlet—not fast enough.

Does that make me a bad person, because I live by ghetto building codes? The only sirens I hear are the paramedics after bodies are bloated sky high, smelling worse than feces pie, lining the fractured sidewalk. Left by some junkie who shot a dose so bad that diarrhea set in before their final sigh.

The incorrigible buildings excoriate me as I pass them by: abandoned factories, stripped of conscience/copper wire—stories of prohibition, World War II tanks, replaced by skanks turning tricks on former assembly line cranks.

Drug deals go bad, or good depending on the attitude and economic livelihood. Crack flakes sell like diamonds in the bush, heroin for the hardcore drinkers that crave a more degenerate thirst.

Arsonists make the Statue of Liberty proud with their torch of indifference, falling embers—comets in the sky, fragmented glass explodes like shrapnel in a war zone—hood-like—jihad.

III.

There are times I don't go out for days, keep the lights off, trigger pulled back. Buckshot into ruby colored trophies, walking dead insomniacs. Bam-bam there goes a thug—thud! Two hundred dollar Jordans, dripping, lifeless. Morgue queued up; crypts are endless: curtain one, two, or three; "Let's Make A Deal."

The intricate, Gothic architecture of Detroit's heyday has become mere mausoleums of noxious lead. Brick by faded brick, basements become violent urns, defaced cabinets displaying decapitated urchins.

Pay your last respects to the faded chalk lines from the last 17 and counting. Neighborhood watch, ammunition going mach one on the next fool that takes a walk down my block. Building code violation—urban tumbleweeds chased by emaciated, demonic pit-bulls, stained a macabre red. Shh. . . can you hear the buildings whisper their decaying despair? Unwilling accomplices who really don't care if they see your face. . . Welcome to the neighborhood. . . Will this be your final resting place?

Marcellus Earl Phillips
Shipwrecked

Merriam-Webster defines "life" as "the quality that distinguishes a vital and functional being from a dead body or inanimate matter; a state of an organism characterized especially by capacity for metabolism, growth, reaction to stimuli, and reproduction." "Death" is simply "the end of life; the cause of loss of life; a cause of ruin; destruction; extinction."

What happens when a person is removed from everything that, to them personally, encompasses what Matthew McConaughey once said was "L-I-V-I-N"?

As I saw it at the time, life was time with my son Adam, sluttery, Adam, concrete, Adam, concerts, Adam, frequent visits with parents and grandmother, Adam, Birch Edge Amusement Park, Adam, Fleming Arrows baseball, Adam, University of Mendoza Marmots football & basketball, Adam, living with one brother and stopping in to see the other at will, Adam, Kiwi Strawberry Snapple, Orange Hi-C, Captain Morgans & Coke, Adam, meat lover's pizza, cheeseburgers, tacos, cheesy bread, sausage & cheese omelettes, Adam, bong tokes, Adam, constant motion, excitement, Adam.

Flyleaf once said, "I won't be satisfied with okay. I won't be okay with alright." Switchfoot once said, "We were meant to live for so much more [before] I made a mess of me." I knew neither of these prophets before things moved forward to the point where my perspective had been vastly altered by the retaliation of society. The elements that define life for me have ceased to include an attitude of sluttitude and inebriants. Those have been superseded by a desire to pursue honor and expiation. The rest of the aforementioned list remains, albeit to greater or lesser degrees.

Stuck in a holding pattern for almost a score of calendars erases vitality. Having no value to the general public, holding no responsibility, and doing nothing constructive with one's abilities is as dysfunctional as I can comprehend. The lack of viable positive encouragement engenders only a degradation of social dexterity. This has catalyzed my devolution from optimist to realist.

"Hope" is "to desire with expectation of fulfillment." The requisite stimulus to nurture emotional wellbeing or health does not exist within these fences.

As a prisoner, am I alive? Stranded between life and death? Or in the vernacular of Monty Python have I "ceased to be"?

Time is a precious commodity. Wasting this gift of merely killing decades is tantamount to hawking a loogie in the Creator's eye. Juxtaposed to the stasis, I would prefer to depart this body and start the celestial epilogue of this narrative at the author's earliest convenience.

Dylan Pruden
This Means Something

Once, when I was a kid, this shrink told my dad I took things because I was trying to steal back some of the love we lost when my mom left us. I don't know. Maybe.

Dr. Robin was about 400 pounds and had this roll of fat hanging from her chin that seems to choke her words when they came out. Vienna sausage fingers come out of a family-sized bag of cheesy poofs and she sucks the orange cheddar dust from them. "He's trying to fill some hole," she says as the wrapper comes flying off a king-sized Snickers. "He feels empty," she says, a spiderweb of caramel hanging from her bottom lip. "Taking things from other kids helps with this." She leans back and punches her hand into a gallon-size jug of Jelly Bellies. The springs in her office chair go spraaaang as if someone has snipped or detuned a piano wire. We all need something I guess.

Today? Standing here in a department store in the burbs, the jewelry and portable electronic devices stuffed in my shirt don't feel so much like longing as they do lust. There's a cigarette hanging from my bottom lip and mostly it's there for companionship. Thinking back, this is affair with nicotine is the closest to a healthy relationship I can remember being in in a long time. The woman at the service counter is eyeing me cautiously as if I'm dynamite, as if she can actually see a digital counter with multicolored wires curlicuing out of it. Her khakis are worn and frayed where the pocket meets the seam and look as if they once fit better. Today? They hang like rags on sun-bleached bones.

"You can't smoke in here," she says in the vapid way younger people mistake for identity. A person like this? I look at her, let the butt fall to the floor and stub it out with my toe. Now, next to a big pink island of bubblegum there stretches an archipelago of graphite-colored burn marks bearing south to southeast. In the way fossils tell a secret story of the past, commercial carpet can be a history—in much the same way the woman's pants relate a lifetime of resignation and servitude.

Walking fast towards the car Brian says, "In Islam they probably kill us for this." Ryan is built like a Y from too many push-ups and pull-ups on the prison yard. Some squats and lunges wouldn't kill him. He has the kind of grunty, squinty face you see on people at the nutrition and sporting goods stores, as if the expression from his last set of seated rows has somehow been permanently imprinted on his face. "Of course," he says as a laptop falls out of his coat and onto the floor next to the accelerator, "in most Muslim countries, for rape you pay what's basically the equivalent of a parking ticket."

I don't need perspective. I don't need erroneous or overly generalized explanations of Sharia law. What I need is a toss up between the new iPhone or possibly another cigarette.

"But here in the good ol' U.S. of A.," he says, as two watches come out of his front pocket, "they have insurance. Did you know that if the insurance industry crashed, the American economy would crash? Hell, as a patriot, it's my duty to steal."

In Southwest Detroit there is a man who buys every computer and computer component we get our hands on. In Del-Ray, an old lady with a giant blue tarp over her roof buys eight-packs of AA batteries by the hundreds. Near Corktown some hipster wants cough medicine—all of it. Ryan has fences that he can go to from the edge of Grosse Point to well into Dearborn.

"All these people have one thing in common," he says as he heaves a mound of couture jeans he's pulled from a rack at a retail chain onto the counter of a pawnshop in the north end. "They're all powerless against greed. If you give someone a good enough deal," he says, "they'll buy anything."

On the way to my loft of Cass Avenue he checks his PayPal account on the tablet he's undoubtedly stolen from one of the millions of retail outlets around the metro area. On Craigslist he sells $1,000 ski jackets for 50 bucks. On Quibids he offers 168 canisters of baby formula for $2.17 apiece. On eBay he accepts a bid of $17 for a 60-inch flat screen.

"You could post a car. I don't know, price it at five bucks. Thing is, nobody's gonna ask any questions," he says.

In America? Right now? This inability to resist the lure of the proverbial free lunch, this desire to endlessly devour things, this is voracity? This is the same gluttony that causes diabetes and bankruptcy.

Upstairs, Ryan says, "Christ it's cold in here." That's because there's no heat at my house. Electricity and water are my sole connection to the grid. Not having someplace warm to sleep isn't so much a conscious decision to withdraw and detach as it is a constant. Like cigarettes, the cold is just another type of security blanket. Winter is the one thing that's dependable and definite that you can fight. It's always there. You can rail against institutions like the gas company till the cows come home, but it eventually they'll just turn off service, put a lock on the meter and go about their business. The fight's not even fair!

"I'm hungry. Whatta ya got?" Ryan cranks the knob to the front burner on my stove. Of course there's no wispy hiss of gas. He opens the oven and looks inside. There's no Sunday pot roast with broasted potatoes and baby carrots. What sits on the greasy rack with stripping stalactites of carbonized chicken fat is a three-inch stack of 10s and 20s rubberbanded together and looking eminently out of place. Ryan tosses that money on the counter. He says, "You have hardly anything in your apartment. The first place someone would look for valuables is the oven. I mean, just from the standpoint of options."

He roots around my cupboards like a tweeker, like a crackhead. With his black cargo pants and his dark peacoat, he looks like a D.E.A. agent on a raid. What he needs are big white block letters on his back that spell out some bureaucratic and militaristic anagram like H.A.L.T. or S.M.A.S.H. He reaches into an open box of Captain Crunch lying on a shelf and pulls out a big fist full of cash with a few Crunch Berries stuck to it. "Better," he says and munches a berry, the crunch conspicuously missing. "But again, where else you're going to put it? Right?" In the refrigerator there is a brick of cheese slices back in the corner next to a half loaf of bread and $688 in small bills. Ryan pushes the money aside and brings the cheese and bread out. Ripping a moldy crust from the bread he points to the fridge and says, "Come on man, you're not even trying."

The thing about camouflage is that it only works perfectly when you're not really looking. When someone hides something, you have to assume—despite evidence to the contrary—that they care about it. This money? It isn't a means to an end. This money? It's ornamental and figurative. It's a derivative and a consequence.

Ryan nailed a light post head on while trying to escape the

parking lot of a big box electronic store, so the next day when he honks his horn out front it doesn't sound so much like a beep as it does a bonk. Downstairs, when I let him in, a girl gets out of the front seat with her head down and walking the way you do when you get up in the morning. She's very thin and has stringy, mouse-colored hair that falls and hides the side of her face a little bit. It looks as if an enormous machine has stretched and elongated her like the kid who was wrung out in Wonka's chocolate factory. She's wearing a dark business suit and a trenchcoat. What she looks like is a lawyer. She's not pretty, but no one going to say, categorically, that she's ugly. Ryan doesn't introduce us, but when he speaks to her he calls her Kayla.

Circling my mattress he raises his tablet into the air or holds it at his waist, trying, with modest success, to filch a Wi-Fi signal from one of my neighbors from the college across the alley. "Listen, here's the plan," he says as if we've ever planned anything. "My 'sources' (he actually makes finger quotation marks) tell me the mall on Big Beaver Road is wide-open. The man who works the video room has been summoned to circuit court for assault with intent to do great bodily harm on a customer he caught trying to steal a giant pretzel from the cart in the middle of the mall. They got a Tiffany's, a Saks and a Macy's. If you can't hit a lick here, you're in the wrong line of work."

Work is a strange word to use.

Ryan balances on the white sill of my front window with his tablet pressed to the glass pane as he takes orders from his fences for Cartier watches. His perch is dicey, the internet connection sketchy, but Ryan's athletic and determined. He chats online with a Chaldean store owner about the possibility of selling him a box of Ralph Lauren polos. He swipes and swipes and swipes through pages of his postings. Things are selling. Gears are turning. The black market, today, is doing what it does. Commerce, in all its myriad forms, can be ambiguous.

Kayla sits on the edge of my bed in front of the one space heater. Her hands are pressed between her knees, and she doesn't talk. She looks cold and more than comfortable with reticence. What you find with people is that they want to tell you things. Even without words, you'll get the point. Most of the time, you have to appreciate anyone who's ever filled a good story, or written an accurate biography for simply saying what's what in the way that isn't too esoteric or cryptic.

On our way out to the mall, sitting in the front seat, every time Kayla flicks the ash from her cigarette out the window, it blows back and disintegrates in my face.

On our first haul I score two bottles of Burberry cologne; a Bose stereo you set your phone on that plays in digital surround sound, takes your pulse and calculates caloric intake; plus I found a nice shirt at Chanel. I put it all in the back seat. Ryan dumps eight smart phones and an obsolete netbook in front. Kayla walks up smiling. It looks weird when she does it, like a scary clown. She's carrying a long duffel bag with a huge Nike swoosh across it. Inside are hundreds of pairs of panties and bras from a nicer lingerie store.

Emboldened we go in for more.

Us? We take racks of suits and shelves full of ties. We sneak an entire display of timepieces. Purloin computers and Xboxes. Take coats from the leather store. Pilfer scarves and cufflinks from the accessories department. We run through the stores like barbarians, like the Mongols, like berserkers. Shoplifting is to us as pillaging is to Vikings. Customers shop, self-absorbed and we mock their fealty to capitalism and this is absurd social contract they honor which compels them to pay for what can so easily be taken. Together the three of us examine ownership and consider objectively what does it mean exactly to possess something?

Kayla comes out with two paper shopping bags filled with Baccarat crystal rocks glasses. Brian has more laptops. I have more jewelry. This stuff? It means something to somebody. A pair of Cordovan wingtips? From Florsheim? Some people find this type of footwear fashionable. A shirt with parrots on it? Tommy Bahama? Some people find this stylish.

Right here? Standing in this encroaching parking lot, this creeping desert of asphalt, this rapidly expanding universe of blacktop? Right now?

We are sated.

Here, the hole is filled.

Kayla says, "Ryan you were right. This place is a gold mine. I'm going back for one more." Ryan smiles like the devil, like the evil genius.

"There's a Gucci store by the Food Court," Kayla says. "There's a J. Crew by the big fountain," she motions vaguely toward the brown brick of the mall. "There's a Crate & Barrel! Let's go!"

Ryan sticks his hand through her open coat and runs it around her negligible waist. It goes down to her thigh and lifts the hem of her skirt a few inches. All this boosting has made Ryan and Kayla a little turned on, a little talkative. "We should definitely hit the Foot Locker too," she says and smiles. Ryan's hand cups the back of her sinewy thigh where the stocking turns darker just below her butt cheek. There is a run in the nylon. He smiles at me and raises his eyebrows as if to say, "Not bad, eh?" As if he owns her and thus has the authority to give her away. She seems too thin for sex, too frail for the physical act. But this means something to somebody. Bonyness? Some people find this body type alluring. Emaciation? Some people find this look very appealing.

Kayla catches me frowning at the empty space between the back of her knee and where the hose comes away from her leg. It looks like a chicken skin stretched over toothpicks. It looks like uselessness. She pushes Brian away and closes her coat tight around her body as if she could ever cover that strange waifishness. "One more for the road, right?" She says looking to Ryan for an answer. The car is packed with stolen merchandise. A speaker tower sticks out the back window. Suits and electronics are mounded over the package shelf. The floors are piled with cell phone accessories and computer games. There isn't room for another thing. There's barely a spot left for me. All this stuff? This effluence? It has significance. It means something to somebody.

After one more lap around the endless galleries and arcades of Summerhill Collection, after one more tour through the land of milk and honey, by complete coincidence, the three of us end up in the same sterile looking Apple Store. Of the six people in the place, three are about to shoplift, two are disinterested and boredly shopping, and one smells of coffee breath and convenience-store cologne. Of the six people in the place, one is an off-duty cop, two are civilians, and three are what you could call anti-civilians. The thing about camouflage is that it only works perfectly when you're not really looking. When someone steals something, it's usually assumed that it was prized, worshiped or venerated by its owner or keeper.

Kayla turns toward a wall of Swarovski crystal-encrusted smartphone cases. They slide off the rack and disappear like Bicycle playing cards up a tuxedo sleeve, like doves under a silk scarf, like a pea under half a walnut shell. Ryan grabs more junk. He grabs the things people don't want anymore. The things that will end up in a box in the basement. These things? They meant something last year. This stuff? One day it'll have kitsch.

Me? Right here? Right now? I can't help myself. The iPhone is metaphorical. It's allegorical. It's analogous. It's a cliché. And it sits on the counter next to the register looking like oversized Legos. Ten of them stuck in a pyramid with their little white logos on the box, which will always remind me of my dad's Beatles records.

The clerk ducks in a little door behind the sales desk to quickly sneak a moment's respite from the hoard of shoppers that threatens to consume everything in its path including himself. Hooking my arm, I steam shovel the bricks into a courier bag freshly liberated from Coach. They're heavy. They have the kind of density you'd expect from bricks. Bricks of gold. Silver ingots. Little bars of platinum. This mess has significance. This weight is substantial.

So, imagine the apocalypse is coming and you've contracted the same virus that's destroying the rest of the world. Suppose that one of its symptoms, part of its pathology, is an acute sensation of vacuous nothing in the chest that, if left untreated, will slowly consume the organs inside your ribcage until you're nothing but a hollow automaton. Pretend that you broke into the CDC and stole the one remaining dose of secret serum that will restore you to health. Now, all you have to do is fight off the Special Ops guys and the horde of Empty Chest Zombies that surrounds you to get out. Let's say this is another analogy. Let's pretend it's one more metaphor, set squarely on your nose, salient and tired. Let's assume it means something.

The cop turned from the display of Bluetooth earpieces. We haven't been especially stealthy, but he knows something's up the way I know he's a cop. His push broom of a mustache is perfectly trimmed and seems to dominate the room. He says, "Alright, drop the merchandise. What are you guys doing?" He seems embarrassed. But, they're always embarrassed for you. I thought for a second keep just might let us go to avoid any further uncomfortability, except under his windbreaker there is a radio that he thumbs. He says, "One eleven at six." Ryan and Kayla drop the things in their hands and run into the mall and disappear.

Me? Right here? Mesmerized by all of this high-end phone gadgetry? I'm trapped. A football field of 3M Duralast carpet tiles between me and freedom. You see those Slurpee stains? You see that baby puke? Commercial carpeting can tell a story in much the same way a big old cop 'stash can evoke vigilance and conservatism. He says, "Don't do it son. We'll catch ya." The thing is, when you get away with something for so long, you start believing you're invincible. If history has taught us nothing, it's certainly shown that with a reasonable amount of heart and daring, it's possible to get away with almost anything.

Officer Mustache and I circle a Formica counter full of limited edition Hello Kitty iPhones like cats. No—Lions! We stop and face each other. Now he's trapped in back, he's the man out. His eyes are imploring. "Whoa, whoa," he says making a patty motion with his hands. "Just whoa there for a sec." Poor officer Mustache. He only wants to arrest me and be done with the whole sordid thing. But he knows. He knows I'm going to shoot out of that door the way I know he doesn't want to chase me. But he will. He will because the cop world expects some effort, and, of course, the criminal code absolutely mandates that I go out in a blaze of glory.

Running through the mezzanine I throw a Tiffany choker over my shoulder. It hits Officer Mustache in the chest. "Here, you want this crap?" I say. "Have it." Zigzagging through the faux-Italian palazzo in the middle of the mall, I yank the Mont Blanc pen set from under my shirt and toss it behind me. It whizzes past his face. "Hold on, there's more," I tell him. A uniformed security guard catches up to him, then passes. For a second, Mr. Mustache can't decide if he should stop and pick this stuff or continue to give chase. "Take this shit," I say laughing. "Trust me, it'll never make you happy." Irony? Some people find it humorous. Sarcasm? A lot of people find it a real hoot. Satire? Some people are just so friggin' impressed with how clever it can be. Me? I tear through the Kiosk Kourtyard and whip gold Davidoff lighters at him. One pegs Mustache right between the eyes.

Lighter is to forehead as bullet is to brain.

Two more rent-a-cops join the chase. I lift my shirt and shake. Timepieces and tennis bracelets are flowing to the ground. Passing through the heavy glass double doors to the parking lot I yell, "That's everything! Take it! It doesn't mean anything!!!" My voice, demented and maniacal, echoes back through the food court, past the valet booth and then over the rows and rows of cars outside.

Here? in this never-ending kingdom of concrete and parking blocks, this textbook example of suburban sprawl? Me? I'm empty. Drained. I'm purged.

My pockets, that is.

Down the infinitely long line of armored personnel carrier-sized sport utilities, Ryan's late-model sedan pulls out of its spot in row triple-Z. I throw my hands in the air and scream, "Wait!" Running, I believe, out of desperation and a sudden unlikely impulse to hope in the hopeless, that I might be able to reach, then loop my arm through the luggage rack and hitch a ride on the bumper. But in the instant the white of his reverse lights turn to the severity of red running lights, I meet a pair of eyes in the rearview mirror. Smiling eyes. Mischievous eyes. Eyes that are slightly sunken from not eating. They're not pretty eyes, but no one's going to say, categorically, that they're ugly. The way Kayla slams the car in drive, the sound the linkage makes as it glides home—this is her laughing. The way the grit on the blacktop crunches as the tires roll over it, the way they squawk when they gain traction and shoot the car up and out, this is her giving me the finger. What you find with people is they want to tell you things. Even if they don't use words, you'll get the point. Giving credit where credit is due, you have to love a good tweet. Ideally, it's just a noun, a verb, and sometimes an adverb: Me? Kneeling? Realistically? I'm spent. Gassed out. Cashed in.

My lungs and thighs and calf muscles, that is.

Me? Right here in row triple-Z? Right now, with salty snowmelt soaking my knees and fingers laced behind my head? I'm getting arrested.

With jail, it's not so much the bad food or the cold cells that break you, It's the lack of stuff. There are no Galaxy S6 Edges, no small-batch True Religion jeans, no artisan-curated jewelry collections, no 32GB Android tablets to possess. There's just you and your thoughts. See what I mean? You see the point I'm trying to make? This Stuff? This shit… it… hell, you get the picture.

When I finally made it back home after posting bond, I found my house has been ransacked. You? You can never be able to tell. But me? Standing here in this Lake Bonneville Salt Flats of an apartment, this liquidated warehouse of the loft, I knew. All my money was gone. When someone steals something, you got to assume it was prized, worshipped or venerated by its owner or keeper. In a garbage-picked novel by Victor Hugo sitting on the floor by my bed, someone has taken the six fresh $100 bills stuck right at the point a Frenchman is jailed for stealing bread. To eat! In a book I picked up from the free box at the used bookstore and takes place in czarist Russia, someone has removed the five fifties I put it right where the poor comrade is having a great moral dilemma with murder. These books? These ideas? This money? Once, it may have meant something.

Outmoded lit is to my apartment as good grammar is to the blogosphere.

Next to my books there is a slip of paper with phone numbers and dollar amounts tallied up in neat little columns. It's not pretty handwriting, but no one's going to say, categorically, that it's ugly. There's also a pair of pantyhose balled up next to some price tags clipped from undies that came from a nicer lingerie store. There is a run in the nylons. People will? They'll tell you things. Even without words, you'll get the point.

Me? If you're asking.

Right now? If you care to know.

I'm exhausted. Weary. Beat.

This? This means something.

Justin Rose
Escape from the Pain
(*Edited for length.*)

My father dropped me off at the middle school around 7:30 a.m.
That meant that I had about eight hours to get wherever I was
headed before my dad got home at 4:00. I was living in a small town
of about 6,000 people, and in a roundabout way, everyone knew
everyone. In my town, they had a bus service you could call and
pay for a ride. They would pick you up and drop you off where you
wanted. The farthest out you could go was the town's outer limits.

So the bus dropped me off at a small out-of-service gas station/
repair shop with a pay phone. Inside the service station, I noticed a
group of older men. Their silver-white hair was hard to see through
all the falling snowflakes. Hmmm, I thought to myself, I wonder if
these old guys can give me a bit of advice. Thinking for a moment,
I decided not to ask them for advice. Instead, I would just kindly
ask to look through a phone book if they happened to have one. A
large lump was growing in my throat. I told myself that I had to get
it together and remain calm, so that I would not give away the truth
about running away.

As I walked through the glass and metal door, bells rattled,
announcing to all those inside the shop that I was there. Sure
enough, all eyes were on me. Four guys sat there staring at me in
dead silence. At first, my thought was to turn around and quickly
go back outside, but just as my thought came to me, one of the four
men spoke up. In a strange crackling voice, behind his glasses, he
looked over at me as said good morning and asked if he could help
me with something.

Once again, I was stricken with fear, but I managed to clear my
throat and ask to use their phone book. The man reached under a
counter and placed the book down. Then he asked if I also needed
to use the phone, and I shook my head to acknowledge that I did.
I pulled up a metal stood and behind to flip through the yellow
pages. At least I had figured out who I needed to call—a taxi cab.
This could get me a long ways from this old country hick town, I
thought to myself.

The old men sat there drinking their morning coffee and eating
fresh-baked doughnuts that smelled real good. One of them asked

me where I was headed. At that point, I had to think fast. I said I was calling a cab so that I could meet my grandma. Then the man asked where I was going to meet her. So, I told him that she lived in the next town, which was 10 minutes west from where I was at the moment. This town was bigger. In fact, this town was twice as big as the town I was living in with my dad. I figured he was going to offer me a ride, but I never accepted a ride from a stranger before. Nonetheless, the old man had to be at least 70 years old, with his soft voice and sweet smile, I'm thinking, why would this old man who was my grandma's age want to hurt me?

He told me that he could give me a ride to meet my grandma, and I eagerly accepted with a thank you. He stretched out his hand and introduced himself as Edward, said that I could just call him Ed. I smiled and told him my name was John, even though that was not really my name. Why did I lie to him and tell him the wrong name? Hmmm. . . I guess I figured that it had to be done to cover my tracks. After all, I had already lied to him about meeting my grandma.

Quietness filled the car for several minutes. My eyes were looking out the passenger side window. The entire countryside was covered in a soft blanket of snow. Huge snowflakes continued to fall fast and just as I tried to follow a single snowflake, it would soon disappear from my sight. Silence broke at last. Ed asked me how come my grandma didn't pick me up, and I told him that she can't drive long distances in the snow. I could tell that he was thinking, but he believed my response to his question.

We were almost to my city of destination. I could see the main street ahead. A new joy and a little fear filled me completely. Suddenly, Ed asked me where my grandma lived. I told him to just drop me off at the 24-hour grocery store because I didn't know exactly how to find her house. When we got to the store, I told him I would call her on the pay phone. He insisted on waiting there with me until she arrived, but I told him I would be OK. Then Ed pulled out a business card from his wallet and gave it to me. He told me that I could call him if my grandma didn't show up.

After he drove away, I couldn't believe my lies had gotten me a free ride, and now I was in a new town with a new-found freedom. It was an exciting and very liberating moment for me at the age of 11. I was thinking, no more abuse, no more rules, no more school, and nobody to tell me what to do.

Little did I know at the time, my life would become an ongoing struggle for freedom.

As the hours passed, I wandered around the new town. There were a couple of things I was afraid of, and the main thing that preoccupied my mind was where I would sleep once night came. After all, it was the middle of winter and the last thing I wanted to do was tell someone that I was a runaway.

It grew colder, and it was pitch black outside. I walked several blocks, and then I decided to sleep in a piles of snow behind a fast food restaurant. My backpack was used as a pillow, and that was so uncomfortable, not to mention how I continued waking up through the night, shivering and with my teeth rattling like crazy.

After a dozen different attempts at trying to sleep in the snow pile, I decided to get up and brush off all the snow off me that had accumulated throughout the night. It was now 5:30 in the morning, and the fast food restaurant was just opening. So, I decided to go inside to warm up and eat something.

Before I knew it, I had fallen asleep at a table, and a lady who worked at the restaurant woke me up and she said she was worried I'd be late for school. All day, I hung around the town, and once again I fell asleep at a different fast food restaurant, but this time it was inside one of those enclosed play jungle gyms for kids. As strange as it may sound, I was sleeping really good, despite all the kids yelling. I was awakened by an employee who, this time, was concerned I should be headed home.

I thought to myself, yeah right, I had no home to go to. But I didn't argue with the lady, I just left the restaurant.

Now a new thought entered my mind. . . parents! Does my mom even know that I ran away? Is she worried about where I am? Has my dad even told her? He may not have, seeing as he might look like the bad parent and lose custody over all this. I didn't want my mom to worry, but I couldn't call her either. And I definitely didn't want to go to my dad's house.

It was now the second night, and the snow was coming down at a pretty fast pace. I needed to find a better shelter than the one I had the previous night. As temperatures were falling, I began to get scared. I was really tired and so cold. I wondered how homeless people did this. I had no idea, but I decided to go back to the same place I had slept before. For whatever reason, it felt safe to me, and it was close to the 24-hour grocery store, just in case I had to use the bathroom in the middle of the night. I tossed and turned for several hours until I was too cold to sleep, and around 3 a.m. I started walking to the grocery store to warm up.

Just as I began walking through the parking lot, a car came speeding up behind me. When I turned to look, I saw a white car, and at first I thought it was a police car. I was just about to take off running, when I heard a voice calling out to me. It was my mom, and she was with my grandpa. My mom couldn't stop hugging and kissing me. It was like we hadn't seen each other in years. My grandpa, mom, and I then went to my grandparents' house. Once we arrived, she let everyone know I had been found.

Unfortunately, I had to return to my father's house, where I got beat up for running away. It was such a horrible situation, and there was nothing I could do to get away.

One summer day, I had another chance to run away. My father was gone at work, and his girlfriend had been watching me for several months. Since I had established a trust with her, she left me home alone for 20 minutes one day. So, as soon as she left, I took all the change from my piggy bank—about $5—and ran out of the house to the railroad tracks. They were only a block from my house. I wasn't even sure where the tracks went. All I knew was they were going to take me away from my abusive father and the prison that I lived in.

Hours went by and I was still walking down those tracks, heading nowhere fast. When night came, I decided to sleep in an apple tree in an orchard. The only problem was that every time I drifted off to sleep, I just about fell out of the tree. After several failed attempts, I started walking down a dirt road until I reached a farm house. Because I was lost, I decide to know on the door to use their phone to call my grandparents to come pick me up.

Their dogs started barking as I walked up the front porch steps of the big old farm house. Before I could even knock on the door, a porch light turned on, and the door opened. A lady wearing a pink nightgown was standing there staring at me.

I explained to the lady that I had been walking to my grandparents' home and became lost. She said I could come in and use her phone to call for a ride. I got a hold of my grandma who said that she and grandpa were on their way over to pick me up. As I was waiting, the lady's husband came down to the kitchen where I was and struck up a conversation. He casually asked me who my father and mother were, and I told him my parents' real names. Then the husband said how he knew my dad.

At that moment, I knew it was going to turn ugly, real fast. The next thing I knew, this man was on the phone with my dad, and before my grandparents could arrive, a truck pulled into the driveway. There was my angry father behind the wheel. I don't have to explain what happened next.

As I've grown older, life hasn't gotten any easier. Actually, it seems like it's getting more difficult in many ways. Throughout my teenage years, I made many mistakes. I had poor judgment. I began shoplifting so that I could live independently, and eventually, I was put on probation. I had to pay fines for stealing, but labeled as a thief, no one wanted to hire me. Really, I was caught in a vicious circle. By the time I was 17, I was sentenced to an adult prison for stealing.

Hoy Sabandith
Family

Guarded by glass. Surrounded by a fancy pine frame.

Smiles photographed. Family, what does it mean?

Is it being from a bloodline? Conceived from a mother's womb? A gray bandanna or blue?

The place I found to fill in the void of an absent father—gang life. Working too much to support his family and not making enough time for me and my brother, I hated him for that. For other children, internet games has taken on the roles of parents. They find their similar loneliness from another place in the world. Hashtag. Surrogates.

My mother urinated on herself at work, not realizing she had a mild stroke. A history of heart problems started at 36.

I didn't realize how lost I've become until the day my mother looked me in my eyes and asked me, "Would I kill her and my father if my gang asked me?" Kudos to tattoo tears.

My heart died that day. I knew I was in the game too deep. It was only a matter of when my rivals would come to riddle me with bullets. I left home at 15. To have no home meant no promises, but it also meant, my enemies wouldn't know where my parents lived.

At 12 years old, my youngest sister never had a chance to share her bruises and visions with her brother. I was supposed to be a brother to a little girl, but I took that experience away from her. Sentenced to 22 years because my heart belonged to loose pants and a careless bandanna that pride would spill blood over, babied me into believing family was here.

The little I knew of my own family would continue to grow further away. Resentment was thick as cluelessness that I searched for in the small reminders around my wrist to recall my father's laugh. Rain, will always remain to be my mother's tears staring out the window wondering if her son is alive.

Behind glass. Handcuffed from ankle, belly to wrist. Prisoner of the state. What did this mean to them?

A decade almost two. My parents continued to find me in all the sounds of loneliness prison left me.

While here, I found out my father had brothers and sisters. She died at 46 in Lao. He escaped concentration camp with a friend, my brother and my mother who was carrying me in her belly at the time. He built a raft. Crossed the Mekong River into Thailand where I was born in a refugee camp. Leaving home for him meant escaping rape or death.

The consequence of my parents working day and night was to provide their children with a better life than theirs, did deprive us the experience of sharing time with them. Me, I've given up 22 years of my life with no other purpose than just trying to find a place to belong.

As I sit in the visiting room, waiting to be returned back to my cell, I see it all around . . .

It is when a wife falls asleep on a husband's shoulder exhausted over a long drive coming to see him right after work.

It is when a little sister attaches herself to her brother's leg, hitching a ride to the vending machine to share their experience of buying candy together.

It is ketchup on a grandmother's lips, staining her grandson's cheek as she kisses him. It is the brave looks from mothers and fathers not held back by shame as they look upon their children. Love is genuine because it continues to find us in the most unexpected places.

Family was clear as carefully listening. Like when my mother's eyes filled with that familiar bubble as she spoke about my little sister, telling me how my little sister spoils her daughter with clothes and toys. My mother is fighting so hard to keep from crying as she explains, "I never bought your sister a single toy to play with."

Family. Beyond love to god, and doesn't come with a manual.

Worth getting jumped in for.

Lennon Whitfield
Held in Suspense with a Panoramic View
(Edited for length.)

This is the true account of my out-of-body experience. This is the first of two experience of this kind I have had during the course of my life. Both occurred during near-death events, and in both instances I was held in suspension outside of myself while I watched the sequence of events take place.

It is not my purpose in writing the account to prove the existence of a deity, nor to prove the existence of heaven or hell. Although I am firm in my belief in the afterlife, it is not my intent to claim knowledge of it. . .

In the summer of 1989, I was a vibrant child of age 9, in my 10th year of life, full of energy with a healthy imagination. I was very sure of myself and confident in my capabilities. There was not an activity or sport that I would not try, entering into it with full expectations that I could win, and eager to impress everyone with my abilities and prove myself to be a formidable opponent.

I had several groups of friends that I alternated my time between. I also had several "best friends" where I would keep our activities exclusively between us when we played together. I love to explore. Any activity that would take me away from my immediate neighborhood was a top priority.

I was raised in Lima, Ohio between the ages of 7 and 13. During these years I was known as Leonard, which was a misrepresentation of my first name, Lennon. My mother named me after my father, but to my young ears, that name didn't sound correct, and I felt it to be an embarrassment; so I insisted that all who knew me call me Leonard.

I was of a light brown skin complexion, and on account of my long eyelashes and dimpled cheeks, I was always being told of how handsome I was by my teachers and other adults, who also frequently referred to me as being "bright."

I was raised by a single mother struggling on welfare. The main disadvantage of my childhood was living an impoverished lifestyle. Although my mother was a diagnosed schizophrenic with alcohol dependency issues at that time, it was the lack of any material possessions that cause me the most anger and resentment in my memories.

I was the third of six children by my mother, the majority being girls. It wasn't until I was 8 years old, when my mother gave birth to another son. Although I was overjoyed at finally having a brother, the differences in our age didn't allow me to reap the benefits of having one as a playmate. Growing up in a home dominated by females left me with a strong desire for another male's presence. On account of my mother's inability to find another male companion after separating from my father, I filled that void by making friends. I dedicated myself to spending as much time with friends as possible, and staying away from home as much as I could.

It was in '89 that I met Michael. We had become friends during our summer vacation from school. I can't recall what common denominator we shared in personality that attracted us to one another. There is nothing of interest about Michael that sticks out in my memories. In fact, the kid was totally unremarkable. Being the man who I am today, having been shaped by my life's experiences and the way one's life experiences can shape thinking patterns and understandings, I can't help but wonder if our meeting one another wasn't preordained — preparing my reservations for a future appointment. . .

Once, Michael and I caught a stray dog. It looked to be one of those fluffy, toy terrier type of breeds that are so popular nowadays. We used an extension cord as a leash. There used to be a girl in Michael's class that he disliked; he claimed she was just as ugly as our pet dog. And so, since our dog lacked a name, she was officially given the name Latavia in tribute to his ugly classmate. Latavia had long claws, so we decided she needed to have them clipped. We took a pair of nail clippers and snapped off one of her claws. It bled profusely. We were too young to know about the nature of dog claws, and upon witnessing our dog in pain and distress, we agreed to let her go free. When we untied her, she took off running down the street, crying out loudly the whole way.

It was during the time of these few short weeks that we discovered our perfect hideaway. I had become annoyed by Michael's reluctance every time I attempted to lead him away from the surroundings he and I knew so well. We lived on the south side of Lima and were removed from the other areas of our city. But the south side was the largest side of town, being comprised of several different neighborhoods. As the days passed, we began to venture further into the depths of the south side, until we found its limits. Beyond the more common areas, we found a complex of "project style" single-level apartments. Although we never explored these apartments, we came across a community center built for that neighborhood. But it wasn't the community center that was the object of our attention.

Lying several yards behind the community center was a basketball court. It was nothing noteworthy. It was just a small section of pavement with a simple goal post. But going further beyond, we found a large pond. It became our everyday practice to walk through that field in the back of the community center; we would each have our basketballs with us, dribbling and chitchatting away.

The day always began at the basketball court, playing several games of "21." Once we exhausted ourselves, and the heart of the day became too much to bear, we would move on to "our" pond, for crawdad fishing and splashing each other in the shallow part of the water. For several days we enjoyed this routine. It became the highlight of our days, and what we looked forward to doing in our tomorrows. It was always just me and Michael, no one else ever seemed to venture back there. There entire vicinity of that field, basketball court, pond and woods were totally isolated. We bound each other to secrecy and a vow to keep others away.

This is where our story takes place, on a day like many before it. We were simple kids, doing those things common to children our age. We had no idea of the fate that awaited us while playing at "our" secret pond. . .

It was a day like many before it. The sun shone brightly. The humidity was high. And there were no clouds to be seen. As usual, we followed the protocol of our daily routine, arriving at the basketball court, each with our own ball in hand. After rigorous games of "21" — jumping, running, shooting, fouls and spats of argumentative debates, we headed for the direction of our pond to dry our sweat, calm our exhaustion, and enjoy the coolness of the water.

Now, our pond had two distinctive sections to it. I would liken its shape to a ping pong paddle. Its perimeter was lined with the natural types of growth that accompanies these kinds of waters. There were cattails, pussy willows, lily pads, and long, thick blades of grass obstructing one's view and approach. Because of this redoubtable vegetation, we kept our distance away from this area. The section closest to us was where the water breached out like the handle on the paddle. The first few feet of water were lined with gravel and crawdads rested among its rocks. We always brought containers to hold them in once we caught them. We would often take them home and attempt to cook them in boiling water, imagining we were preparing a delicacy.

It was during this moment, I began to play with my basketball while in the water. I observed that the ball would remain afloat, and would give strong resistance to being submerged. This phenomenon intrigued me, so after experimenting with floating on top of it, I was confident I could use it to float to the other side of the pond. I shared this revelation with Michael, who felt doubtful of my being able to achieve it. He attempted to plead with me not to try.

But I was sure that it could be done and I was going to prove it. I held my ball under my neck and upper chest, with my arms wrapped securely around it. I used my legs and feel to kick, generating a rhythm that propelled me forward. I was doing it! I was swimming! By the time I reached halfway across, my excitement was too much to hold in any longer. I stopped dead center, turned around, and began to make my way back to Michael. I had to tell him to his face, "I told you I could make it!"

Making it back to the shore, we were drunk on the excitement of what I had just done. We decided we would both go across together, each one of us using his own ball. We started out, both of us using the same technique I demonstrated earlier. We were traveling, no longer in the safety of the shore. I remember continuing my "pep" talk, sharing the thrill of my joy with Michael, and the fact that we were "doing" it. But little did I know of the panic that was rising in Michael's mind. The fear of the knowledge that he was now in the cater of the water must have overwhelmed his reason. He went mad. . .

In one fluid motion, Michael released his ball, and jumped on my head and back. He was screaming, "Leonard, save me!" while attempting to hold himself above the water by using me as his floatation device. The suddenness of his move caused me to lose hold of my basketball. It popped out of my grip like a cork being shot out of a bottle. Neither of us could swim and now we no longer had anything to keep us afloat.

Michael was in a hysterical panic, beating me in my head and back with his arms and legs. I was swallowing big gulps of water while struggling to get my head above the pond for air. Every time I managed to break the surface, Michael was able to climb on top of me, forcing me back under. I felt panic! I knew I was going to die.

Suddenly, in an instant, I was standing outside of myself. I was held, suspended in the air, several yards above the pond. I had a panoramic view of the scene that played out below me. I was able to see with clarity the struggle for life that Michael and I were in. I could see the contorted expressions on his face as he beat the water with me struggling underneath him. In those moments that I stood outside of myself suspended in the air, I felt a great calm take over me. I no longer felt afraid. I felt indifference to the scene I was now witnessing.

It was during this great calm that I allowed myself to discontinue my struggle. I no longer fought against Michael or tried to break the water for air. I allowed myself to drift into the depths. I remember looking toward the sky and seeing the rays of sunlight dance through the surface.

Before I knew it, my feet were touching the sand below. I could feel its slimy, gritty texture sliding through my toes. Just as suddenly as I had stood outside of myself only seconds before, now I became acutely aware of my situation and my need to get out of the water. I still felt no panic, though now I felt the urge for air. I slid my arms out before me and swam backward against the water.

Finally, my head broke the surface and I was able to climb out. I sat on my butt with my knees drawn up to my chest, my arms wrapped tightly around them. There I sat, unmoving, while I watched my friend Michael continue to drown.

He repeatedly called out to me, "Please, Leonard, save me!" I could hear the sound of him swallowing water with every yell.

Finally I could stand it no longer: It was time for me to save my friend. . .

I walked out into the water until it was up to my nose. I took a breath, then walked until the water covered my head. I held my right hand extended in Michael's direction. I felt his hand grab a hold of mine. After a couple of attempts, I was able to pull him in.

On the shore of the pond, we both sat recovering from our ordeal. Neither of us spoke. At some point my thoughts came back into focus. I saw Michael's ball drifting in the water; my ball was resting among the rocks on the other side. Being at a loss for words, I stood up, grabbing my container of crawdads. I walked to the other end of the pond, retrieved my ball, and without missing a beat in my stride, I proceeded through the field in the direction of home.

During the course of my departure, I heard Michael's steps running to catch up with me. He came to be walking in stride alongside me. I remember feeling annoyed by this. Even though I didn't speak it, our friendship was over. The only thought that played through my mind, "Michael had just almost caused me to drown. . ."

To the best of my recollection, I never knew what happened to Michael beyond that day. Michael and I never played together anymore. We most certainly never ventured back to "our" pond. This is a story I don't recall telling to anyone before. Why that is so, I cannot say. It's just one of those mysteries, like the many that occurred during our near-drowning experience.

Benjamin Yoder
A Demonic Alliance

He awoke all alone in the midst of a dark forest. His skin was cold and clammy. He wore no shirt, shoes or socks and only a pair of ragged jeans covered his lower half. He was clueless as to where he was, how he got there or where he was headed. Nevertheless, he began to walk in hopes of finding the clearing.

During his journey, he encountered numerous obstacles. He was attacked by vicious demons and harassed by evil spirits that cast bad medicines, illusions, and mental anguish upon him. He thought about fighting back, but his adversaries were very powerful. He himself was a strong warrior, but her thought that a man alone would be no match for an evil war party.

When he came to believe that he was incapable of fighting these evil forces, he attempted to retreat. He ran for hours at a time, stopping only for a quick wink of sleep from time to time. Sadly, no matter how far he ran, the others would find him and continue their attacks. Moreover, the darkness was everlasting, so he never knew they were coming until claws were tearing the flesh from his skull and digging into his brain. Giving up was not a realistic option as they always left him alive. . . barely. For death was not their intent, they preferred to make him suffer.

One day, as he lay battered, bloody, and hopeless against the bitter forest floor, he was approached by a pair of twin demons. They were the first things he'd been able to see during his time in the forest as the outlines of the two glowed like neon lights though the rest of their bodies were as dark as the nightmare they inhabited. As he braced for yet another attack, he was surprised by four outstretched arms lifting him to his feet.

"My name is Al," remarked demon number one. "My brother Dru and I have come to offer you our protection."

"How could only the two of you protect me from the plethora of evil in this forest?" he asked the twins. "There are swarms of them, and it's too dark to see them, let alone fight them."

"We are more powerful than any demon in this forest," remarked Dru. "The others want no part of my brother and I, and if you'll accept our offer, it will be as if they do not exist."

"What good will that do me if I'm still trapped in this miserable forest?" he asked. "Furthermore, you're demons just like them! Why would you help a man such as myself? Tell me, what are you to gain from your offer"

"We only ask one thing in return for our assistance," replied the twins. "Just promise that you'll keep us by your side no matter what. That's it. You do that, and we'll guarantee your safety as well as an eventual departure from this forest."

"I don't know," he replied. "What sort of trouble am I asking for by befriending twin demons? Why should I believe you?"

"What could be worse than the torture the others have put you through? We're offering our help. If it's not appreciated then we'll leave you to the others. Take it or leave it!"

"Okay, okay, I'm sorry," he replied. "I didn't mean to seem ungrateful. You have my word. I'll keep you with me and call upon you whenever the others attack."

"Then, we have a deal," replied the twins. "Let us walk the forest."

So Al and Dru led him around the forest for what seemed like an eternity. He was glad to be protected from the others, but as time went on, he began to suspect the twins were as evil as they. He wanted to find a way out of the forest and back to his family, but it seemed as if the twins were leading him in the opposite direction. For every time he felt a clearing or heard the calls from his family, the twins would convince him to go a different way.

As time dragged along, the night got darker and the forest got thicker. As the climate got progressively worse, he became increasingly frustrated with the twins. They were leading him deeper in the forest, and he could no longer hear the calls from his family.

"Am I ever going to get out of here?" he roared at the twins. "All we've been doing is running in circles!"

"Just trust us," replied the twins in unison. "You said you'd take our advice, so come on. It won't be long now."

As he felt his way through the forest, he arrived at a spot that was void of trees.

"Is this the clearing?" he thought to himself. But, the air was still pitch black.

"Why is there no light?" he demanded. "Is this the clearing or not?"

"Um. . . just stay put for a while," replied the twins. "The light may come yet."

As he stood there in the void, he came to realize that Al and Dru were exactly what he suspected. They were tricksters. There would be no light, and the place he stood was indeed not the clearing. All of these thoughts were validated the second he tried to move only to discover he'd sunk to his waist in quicksand.

"Help," he exclaimed. "Al, Dru, pull me out of here. . . PLEASE!"

"Sorry," they chuckled in unison. "We never agreed to protect you from the elements, only the others."

As he stared daggers up toward the outlines of the twins, evil neon grins blazed a trail across each of their jawlines.

"To hell with the both of you," he shouted as he reached out to grab the branch of a glowing cedar tree. "Go on now! Get away from me, I don't need you!"

"Now, now," the twins replied in unison. "If we leave you here, the others will surely tear you apart, and you'll be most defenseless buried up to your waist in quicksand."

"I'd rather face the others than spend another minute with you phonies!" he replied. "I'll fight them on my own, and I'll keep fighting until I find the clearing myself. You are nothing to me! You are fake! Poison! Go on, be gone! Stay gone! GRRRRAAAAHHHH!!!"

As he began to pull himself from the muck, he belted out a mighty growl; a deep, but musical growl, so loud that it shook the forest, knocking trees to the ground in every direction. His booming howl echoed and carried through the trees for what seemed like an eternity, a warcry ever long.

He ripped himself from the muck, leapt to his feet, and began to charge the twins in a vicious and unyielding frenzy of wild rage. As he neared the glowing outlines, tiny slivers of light began to slash through the treetops. As the beams crashed against the twins, they instantaneously burst into smoke like hot coals doused with water.

When he realized the twins were gone, he knew the others would come after him. He put his head down and began to run with all his might toward the sunlight that sneaked through the trees. But, suddenly, he stopped running, lifted his head and clenched his fists.

"No." he said to himself. "No more running. I said I would fight, and that's what I'm going to do."

He looked down to his left hand and noticed he'd been holding a stalk of cedar from the glowing tree. He clenched the medicine tight in his hand and lifted it toward the sky.

"Creator, I need you!" he called out. "Please. . . give me the strength to fight these demons and to stick it out at any cost. I don't want to be a quitter. I want to be a winner, but I can't do it without you. Please. . . Guide me!"

He placed the cedar back to the earth and began to walk confidently toward the light, and the beams grew stronger with each step he took. As he looked ahead on his newfound path, he noticed that the others were rapidly approaching, but through the beams of light, he could see the demons for what they really were. His fear was gone, and for the first time since he awoke in the forest, he felt as if he were in total control.

"I see you now," he roared at the others. "I'm not afraid of you anymore! You're just an illusion! You are too weak, and I am too strong! Come on, bring it on!"

He lunged toward the war party of evil with a killer instinct. Before he knew it, he was trading blows with some of the forest's most powerful demons. With every punch he threw, and every hit he took, the once tiny slivers of light began to explode into blinding infernos. As the militant beams crashed against the army of evil, they began to fall one by one. Soon after, they each burst into flames, burned to ashes and were spread through the air by the unforgiving winds of the cold, dark forest. The others were gone.

Though battered and painted with the bloodstains of battle, he continued on his path with his head held high. He looked up ahead on his path and he could see the clearing: a luminous plot of serenity. After he reached the clearing, he began to rest and to allow his road to recovery to commence. He looked much further ahead on his path, there were his parents, his siblings, aunts, uncles, nieces and nephews; his whole family was smiling and waiting.

Again, he looked to the sky: "Thank you, Creator. I am almost home."

Contributors

James Adrian

I wanted to write about myself, but who I am is only defined by how you receive me and my poetry because I am a SOULJAH to the struggle and a SERVANT to the people. I am a JUVENILE LIFER and a CHANGED MAN striving to be BETTER THAN YESTERDAY!

"#SeewhatI'msaying" is about people understanding me before I am gone. I want to express my thoughts so people can see that I am trying to better the world and help those in need to hear my story in an effort to make life easier for them. I don't know why I feel certain ways sometimes, but I know I'm not alone and others experience it too.

"Grandma's House" is about my thoughts and memories as a child. I don't know where my life is going to make me and most of my friends have been family. I didn't have a care in the world and everything was fun. I still had my innocence. I didn't know we were poor or that my family had problems. I just felt the comfort of family, love and acceptance. All of it changed when my Granddaddy died and only my Grandma was still there to hold things together. She is still holding on and she told me that she hopes I'm free before she dies and that hurts my heart, so I try to remember the days at her house and not the days we share on visits once a year.

"How Would You Feel If?" is a chance to look into the life of a prisoner and see how we see things in here. The small things in life we often take for granted until we finally take time to see things for what they are and reality is like a smack in the face in here and it's far from normal.

George Benton

Thank you for this opportunity to display God's gift to so many people throughout the world. Learning and understanding as the years of life continue to be precious. Knowing deep down in my heart if it wasn't for God and my grandmother's wisdom I wouldn't know where my state of mind would be. Seeing how I seen where I come from, now I understand where I am going. Words change the way love receives things, when patience finds how to overcome the struggles in between. The inside of you make the difference not what your circumstances SEE. Love others, love yourself, love what you do, but most importantly USE the gift GOD blessed you in your mother's womb to do. Write.

Charles G. Brooks, Sr.

These pieces are forged from my life experiences. I am a 32-year-old man who was born and raised in Detroit. My aspirations were always loftier than my choices may seem to indicate, but as I reshape my life, I hope my words can influence as many people as possible. I write so that my children can see the world as I saw it, and make the choices that I didn't. I write to purge my soul, because writing is my therapy. "We Were Kings Once" is about the status that crime brought to the average youth in my neighborhood, as well as the often-overlooked consequences.

Demetrius Buckley

Time is in constant motion for me, always advancing and transferring the delicacy of life, that means of leaving when nothing inside or around you can no longer be but quietly exist within the confines of self. Living, to its desired degree, is almost summed up to be a privilege, a prerogative to experience being human or emotionally attached. My poems, in a sense, comes to life in that self where I try to connect the minds & hearts of readers to mine as they begin a journey in the images I paint with the collection of words. Since my youth I had a taste for creating strong images through the rhetorical syntax, and now I crave the well-styled poetry verse as if it were a close friend, or someone I once knew long ago.

Robert Lee Alan Caldwell

My writing is an experiment in expressing universal thoughts and emotions. It is my attempt to bridge the gap between experience and communication. To challenge our preconceived notions of the meaning of language and its role.

Bill Cook

I am a 67-year-old Vietnam war veteran. In the early part of this millennium, I suffered and fought my way back from a series of strokes. Although I have been relegated to a wheelchair, I refuse to relent. During good weather, the track beckons and I readily submit doing a mile or two at a time usually three times daily. While on the track, I find inspiration for a work in progress and even a new one. Writing is a pleasure that takes me away from the negative life of incarceration. I believe that you can incarcerate the body, but you cannot incarcerate the mind.

J. S. Copeman

Having served in the first Persian Gulf War during Operation Shield/Storm, I returned with some mental health issues that caused me great problems, leading to despair and heartache. Now I write as I've been locked up too long and while not shirking personal responsibility, I do attribute my behavior as a matter of exposure(s), mostly to solar radiation, secular existentialism, and the worst of all, the MDOC. Thus tainting my face with lines, my mind with inconsistencies, my eyes with irony, and my soul with despair. So. . . good reader, all I really strive for these days is to tell you what I see and hear as a note behind the blue and orange curtain of corrections. That and maybe add a little criticism (okay, a lot), because it's always about hope in the end. No matter what I say. Hope.

Grant Czuj

The words sometimes escape me, but something they don't, rattling around in my head like the songs one can remember, then forget, then remember again; finding oneself humming or mumbling the lyrics. But these songs or poems or scribblings are unwritten until I scratch them onto a scrap piece of paper, or a napkin, or sometimes the back of an envelope. I don't know where they come from and I don't know where they may be going. Thousands of unread words stashed and pocketed. They sprout from many different triggers and inspirations: smells, sights, memories, old stories, love, anger, deception, lust, etc. . . When I read other work, I can sometimes see myself in it, recognizing that the world is more infinite than I had first believed. Poetry can sometimes be a clear mirror to look into. When seen in a reflection, those words can no longer find an escape.

Chris Dankovich

If a man falls in the woods, and there is no one around to see him fall or hear his cries, was he ever really there?

Marco de'Lor

Hello, people of the Artistic Community. My name is Marco de'Lor. I appreciate your interest and love for Poetic-Expression. That shows anyone can obtain and enjoy the beauty of words. Even a convict. Please embrace my body of work. I truly have lived this road. I only know my walk, but beyond that I know nothing. Of course I'm currently the property of the state. I'm 30 years young and living my legacy with every stroke of the pen. Hopefully one day our paths will cross.

Denver

[No bio available. This is Denver's second appearance in the Review.]

Rebecca Fackler

I've been writing poetry for over 25 years, since I was in my early teens, and I started to write poems about what I went through in my childhood. I was raised in a very abusive family. When you read my poems you'll see the hurt and pain that I endured at the hands of not my father, but other men in my life. But I came through all that I went through not only with my pride and dignity. But the one thing that I can say about myself is that I'm a survivor.

John C. Gaik IV

When I was 11 years old, I won first place in my school's reflections contest. It took me a week to type six pages. Much of the story had to do with the inventions on a spaceship I named, The Michael Jackson. When the astronauts reached their target planet they were quickly killed by a giant spider. That was 1994. I was proud of my story, and still am. My literary tastes and writing style have changed since then, but the fire to that initial spark still burns brighter than ever inside these walls.

Scotty G

As a writing prompt, I was asked to write about where I keep painful memories, and I used that as the seed for this short piece. I struggle with regret and shame every day and wish I could do something to ease the pain of my victim, of the people hurt by my crime.

M.G. Glenn

I started writing when I was 12 years old. I entered and won two "young authors" competitions for my short stories in middle school. Basically, I got older, life got harder, and I made some bad decisions. Now, I write just to get it out of my system. I believe it was Stephen King who said that it was "purge or perish." I definitely get that. So here it is, for better or worse.

Norman Hile

"Death is an Awakening," stated Leo Tolstoy in War and Peace. These words can be attributed to a person who has experienced such a metamorphosis. I as a person have too "awakened" from a "death." As one incarcerated, I now live through reading great literature and by expression of my own into words and prose. I "awaken" to the beauty and scope that language can display inner feelings and external truths. I hope to convey an invocation, to all who read my words, unto parts of themselves previously unknown.

Gabriel Jagniecki

I am a 26-year-old from Stony Lake, Michigan. Writing has always been a good outlet for me to express myself and cope with problems in my life. This summer I've had a great opportunity to spend time with a lot of creative people, play music, write lyrics and keep a journal. The writings I'm sending in are fragments of me and what I've experienced over the past six months. Lately I've fell off writing and been spending more of my time and energy playing music, but the two combined have been a true source of freedom!! I've found a new peace and happiness through relationships based on this creative force flowing through us and using it to learn how to love and care for others. Not always easy, but very worthwhile!

So here is a brief look into a strange mind and even stranger, one of the most conducive summers of my life. These experiences brought me great joy, grief, sadness, but most of all growth, and hopefully I can share that with you guys.

Darnell L. Jett

Born and raised on the west side of Detroit, the importance of self-expression was some that was deeply ingrained in me as a child. By the time I was 11 years old it was settled, I had completely fallen in love with the power of words. And yet, even still to this day, I can't imagine anything more liberating than my thoughts finding their way to a page.

Now, at the age of 28, poetry, along with a few other forms of creative writing have become my way of seeing, and embracing the world around me for what it really is. Not to mention everything I've learned that it's not! So much of who I am goes into the poetry I write. I would say it's my escape, but when I'm writing, it feels as if I'm digging myself deeper into the very fiber of who I really am, other than running in the opposite direction.

Despite the fact that I'm currently incarcerated at this very moment, I still hold onto the hopes that my work could benefit or inspire someone, somewhere, to see things just a bit more clearly if nothing else.

Asia Dominique Johnson

"Whatever happened just had to happen." I heard that in a song and though it seems an elementary line, it resonated deep within me and inspired "Rodale Park."

The past. . . it happened. But now, right here in this moment, what "happened". . . well. . . it happens for me right here on this piece of paper. Every time I write, I refer to it as "The Happening."

"Shit happens" — another famous quote. I thank everyone worth thanking for the fact that in my life, shit no longer happens. I MAKE SHIT HAPPEN!

Thank you for reading. . .

Patrick Kinney

I started writing stories and poems in 1998, three years into a life sentence that began when I was only 16 years old. My work has appeared in several small magazines and most of the previous volumes of MRPCW. My autobiography, All the Rivers Run, is available for a discount on www.lulu.com (all profits are donated to charity,) and its short sequel, Into the Sea, is posted on the Victories blog at www.prisoneradvocacy.org. The MRPCW has been a reason to keep on writing through those "dark, dark days and darker nights."

Floyd E. Kohn

I should tell you a lot about myself, but the poems will tell you all the important things about me. They are pieces of my south and spirit. Unfiltered and off-the-chain like a free slave. Words are my way to emancipation. Every word and how it contributes to the whole verbal picture is a proclamation of sorts. I paint on a canvas of paper. I am in my 30s. I am a fun-loving person. And I love writing. I've been at it since I was 13½ years old. I grew up in Benton Harbor. I went to Coloma High School and I also went to Western Michigan University. I get out of prison in 2017 and I plan on being a published poet and art gallery owner. I live in Kalamazoo, but love to travel and meet new people on a Fear and Loathing trip. And that's me in half a nutshell. I hope you enjoy the poems as much as I do. Enjoy and peace be with you.

Dell Konieczko

I was born on an Indian reservation in North Dakota, but was adopted out to a white family when I was 2 years old. Spent my childhood in California. Came to prison in Michigan when I was 17. I'm 54 now. Still living, trying to learn. Trying to find a place in this world that's comforting, and the justification for being there.

Daniel W. Lee

Daniel Lee is a 33-year-old male. This is his second submission to the PCAP program and he had a short story published in last years' edition.

Diana Lewis

My name is Diana Lewis and I have spent a huge chunk of my life behind bars. Sure, I've been to prison four times, but that's not what I'm talking about. I was locked behind bars of anger, addiction, self-deception, loneliness, sex, money, unstableness, and living life on the edge.

At my lowest point I exploded in criminal behavior which lead to by being incarcerated and to where I eventually discovered freedom. I had to get all of the "noise" out of my mind, so I prayed, I started baring my heart on paper and things started to make sense for the first time in my life. As I began to siphon through the craziness in my life my truths started to come to light and I realized I had been hiding behind many masks, locked behind the very bars that I, myself had put up to keep everyone away so that I wouldn't get "hurt;" I realized I had become trapped behind and by my own design.

As I started to face myself behind MDOC Prison walls, I could no longer blame anyone but me. I had to honestly look at why I was here and get my priorities in order, either I'm going to remain a shell of who I really am locked up for life or I was going to quit running and and truly live. I am willing to tell my story today so there is nobody that can ever say anything about me that I haven't already said, and shown that yes, Alice, you can fall through the rabbit hole and end up in an adventure and still find your destiny!

K.T. Lippert

[No bio available. Mr. Lippert's story collection God Bless America appeared in 2000.]

David Michael Martin

David Michael Martin has written three unpublished science fiction novels totaling 416,000 words and is now searching for a publisher.

The short story "Renoir Goes to Market" went through eight revisions. It is a first person present tense interpretation of the painting To Market by Pierre Auguste Renoir (1841-1919). The story reminds us that a painting is not a picture. It is worth thousands of words—but in viewing it, one cannot see the words, cannot touch them, cannot speak them, cannot hear them, and yet they outlive flesh and blood, waiting only to be felt by the viewer. Only then can they be seen.

Mr. Martin graduated from the Ohio Institute of Technology in 1982 and was an electronic engineer until 1987. He received a Bachelor in Specialized Studies from Ohio University and has completed 36 semester-hours of graduate school from Adams State University to date. Mr. Martin lives in western Michigan.

Corey Joseph Montague

I write as my last line of survival. After 29 years of incarceration I have compiled a catalog of manuscripts and short stories. I'll be released in December of 2020. But without opportunity waiting, or any means of support, I am destined to fail. Even the shadow of my unpublished works will fade into history undiscovered. Serendipitously, if some of my work falls into the right hands I'll become a moderately successful author. If not, it wouldn't have been for lack of trying.

Justin Monson

Am I a writer? Often I find myself asking this question. The affirmative answer I long for evades me. I have this ridiculous sentiment that in order to be a writer one must garner some mysterious set of accomplishments. Publish a book. Be interviewed on NPR. Become an alcoholic. Write 12 hours a day, and proclaim half of it garbage. Move to New York. End up in Connecticut. Then France. Then England. Then Hong Kong. Then Connecticut again. I've done none of these things. I've done NONE of these things.

I need to remember that writers write. Not all of them are published. Not acclaimed. Not sought after by interviewers. But they all write. So, I guess that's what I'll do: Write. Though, if anyone would like to tell me I'm a writer, I'd be cool with that too.

Steven L. Montez

Though I seek more than memories, they are precisely what I recover in greater abundance with each passing year. Among the detritus of these increasingly generic days, I am fortunate enough to find pieces of yesterday hiding among the great emptiness of here and now. Occasionally they appear in stark epiphany. But most of the time I must pick them up and dust and polish them before I can see the me underneath. And the tools that I use in this excavation of my life are wielded in the form of blue Bic pens, cheap lined writing tablets, and a merciful recollection of the moments I have known. Sometimes I find a piece of gold that I foolishly cast away years ago. Sometimes I find a fossil of a life that once roamed freely. But in the dirt beneath these barren moments I always find a reason to write one more piece. One more line. One more word. One more time.

Bryan Palmer

[No bio available. This is Mr. Palmer's first appearance in the Review.]

L. Parker

Writing is a talent I discovered in prison and it will be the talent that will get me out of prison. I love manipulating words in such a way that my readers see, feel, even taste what I say. When I tell a story, I want my readers to experience the feelings I convey— whether it be fear, joy, frustration, hunger or anything.

Marcellus Earl Phillips

M.E. Phillips is the author of an as-yet-unpublished sortabiography titled Sorry Mom and Dad, It's Not Your Fault. Let's be honest, he's a rookie just trying to find his legs in this adventurous world of creativity and kindle the spark of inspiration while maintaining the conviction of living life for bigger and better principles, priorities, and goals. Thank you for sharing a small portion of your day with me. Bless you and all those you hold dear and may the Force be with you.

Steven Pribbernow

I struggled for quite awhile with what to write here, with what to share about myself and my writing. In the end, I figured I'd keep it simple: I started writing poetry when I was 13. I considered it a productive outlet for my inner turmoils. Productive because it got me away from the razor blade. I guess you could say that it saved my life. I've been locked up since I was 15 and, in that time, writing is one of the few true joys I've known. It still holds the same purpose as before, but now it has more meaning to me. I want to be successful at it. Not for the fame (actually I read somewhere that most poets don't become famous until they're dead), but for the personal sense of accomplishment.

The poems I submitted this year are of different styles than what I usually write. Over the past year I've begun to experiment with different poetic forms, sometimes following specific guidelines and sometimes altering the "rules" a little to fit my own style. Or I just create my own form. I think, as writers, we should always try to expand our abilities and so that is what I tried to do this time around.

Dylan Pruden

The hardest part of writing is making someone feel something more than they necessarily understand. "This Means Something" is satire and irony which I purposely overworked because making my point in the subtle or artful way didn't seem to fit the theme, and, regrettably, I'm not that talented. It's about the cause of suffering, ignorant desire and commercialism's vulgarity.

Rik

I have been writing for many years, but have never shared my stuff with very many people. My friend Daniel Turrentine heard some of my stuff and pushed me into entering. I pushed him into the art show so he replied in kind. I thank him for the shove. My poems are like my paintings. I tried to confuse matters so they reflect reality, albeit distorted and broken. I had to sort through the pieces and dig up what I feel about life; pain, confusion, distorted values and loss. That is my reality, so, that is what I write about.

Justin Rose

My name is Justin Rose. I am 30 years old. I was born and raised in Grand Rapids, Michigan. I have a younger sister and older brother. I really love writing short stories, novels, poems, songs and journals. I first started writing at age 9. My dream is to someday get a degree in Fine Arts and become a published author.

In my free time I love listening to music, cooking, reading, writing and being in the Great Outdoors. I'm planning for my future release and a bright future. I feel honor and pride to be a part of University of Michigan's efforts to stop mass incarceration and focus on alternatives to such an out of control problem America has.

Hoy Sabandith

I am just a mother's son who wants to leave something behind that's worth remembering.

Seven Scott

With his newest poems, Seven Scott continues to point readers in interesting directions when he shines a light into the darker corners of his life's experiences, where readers seeking an intelligent, eclectic perspective may mine for nuggets from his introspective self-awareness and prison-based insights and observations. Enjoy!

Dawan Smith

Born and raised in Detroit, Michigan, I was always attracted to literature. Now at age 32, I find liberation in giving voices to the unique perspectives that often go unheard. I began with poetry where I found a flair for storytelling. Although I am currently incarcerated, my intent is to deliver to the world with my unique voice.

Dominique C. Stone

I write to find myself. I write to find within myself what I have hidden from the world, from myself. I am a broken poet; what I cannot explain to myself, to others, I can explain to the pages, through my guitar. I write to embrace the pain and loneliness inside. I befriend it through the possibilities that riddles and rhyme schemes provide. I once heard that "a poem is an emergency of the spirit." What cannot be explained in mere words will always be expressed through the lyrics of our hearts.

Michael Sullivan

[No bio included. This is Mr. Sullivan's fourth consecutive appearance in the Michigan Review of Prisoner Creative Writing.]

Daniel Turrentine

Observing life's ever-unfolding presence compels me to express my shade of reality with others. This is why I write. And maybe my words, in some way or another, will affect others the way that writers previous to now have affected me.

Dennis Vesey

I was born and raised in Ypsilanti by my parents, who I am proud of, and honored to call Mom and Dad. I've been incarcerated since the age of 23. Today I stand erect, saluting the sun at the age of 35.

At a young age, the allure of the streets, and all its promise of glitter and gold, had attractive powers over me. As such, I lived a life that dictated my future. A life that at a glance suggested with high probability that I was capable of murder.

Today I am serving a natural life sentence for a crime that only God, a handful of people, and I know I did not commit. And while this may sound sad, this unfortunate situation had to happen, as its chapter is where the climax in my book of life was written. After 12 years in prison I have now realized that I have wings, I am colorful, I am beautiful—I am a butterfly.

My poem is about the African American evolution, which I believe to have many highs, many lows, but no beginning or ending. Just as all things were, I believe its existence was and is the desire of intelligence that was alive before the primordial hydrogen atom. I have merely attempted to capture a still picture of its existence in a place and space in time that I have fortunately either witnessed or heard of.

Joseph Villarini

I started writing poetry when I was just a child. My grandmother had diabetes and when she didn't feel good, I would write for her in hopes of making her feel better. She always said I had a gift, but she passed away, and I never took my writing seriously. It wasn't until I met the love of my life that I found motivation to write again.

I became more creative because with each poem, I wanted her to feel the love I had for her through my words. I discovered how powerful words can be so I started to expand the basis of my poetry.

I began writing religious poems, poems about alcoholism and drug abuse, the aspects of prison life and our way of thinking that led to incarceration. I soon realized that I was writing the best poetry I'd ever written. People relate to my poetry and some even found inspiration to have different outlooks on life, as well as express themselves through writing.

Being myself, writing about real life events, and expanding my horizons through poetry has emphatically changed my life.

Cozine Welch

[No bio available. Mr. Welch's work has appeared in several issues of the Review and also online in The Periphery.)

Lennon Whitfield

I am a 36-year-old male who's lived an eventful life, full of strife and street experiences. Due to my years of "ghetto" activities, I have recently been compelled to write a chronicle of my memoirs entitled The Revealing of my Naked Soul. The True Memories of a Street Protagonist.

I enjoy writing and bringing my stories to life. Besides that, I'm an artist, specializing in pencil drawing. My goal is to one day share my life's experiences with the world out of my own innate need of finally revealing the truth of who I am . . .

Tanya Willhelm

I have wanted to be a writer ever since I was about 8 years of age. My aunt every Sunday used to put up a little writing station for me. It had a stamped envelope that I assumed was an actual address of a publishing company. I would then create a story and send it out, placing it in her mailbox. It seemed I was always waiting for a reply, which of course never came. My need to create new stories didn't die with her. Instead it grew. I one day hope to create new worlds and terrifying stories to captivate audiences.

Benjamin Yoder

Benjamin Yoder's Anishinaabemowin name is Shkinwe Mko which means New Bear. Benjamin has been incarcerated for the past seven years. However, he is hopeful and doesn't let it define his future. He has been taking college classes for the past four years and has developed a strong passion for writing. Benjamin's career goal is to become a Substance Abuse Counselor.

A Word About the Prison Creative Arts Project

The Prison Creative Arts Project (PCAP) is an organization that opens up opportunities to create original works of art in correctional facilities, juvenile facilities, and urban high schools across the state of Michigan.

Founded in 1990, PCAP is run by members of the University of Michigan and surrounding community and is based in the University of Michigan Department of English Language and Literature. Its programs include the Annual Exhibition of Art by Michigan Prisoners, the largest prison art show in the world; The Michigan Review of Prisoner Creative Writing, the amazing collection of writing you are currently holding in your hands; weekly theatre, creative writing, visual art, and music workshops with incarcerated adults and juveniles, as well as students from Detroit; the Linkage Project, which affirms the creativity of adults and youth returning from incarceration; and the Portfolio project, a one on one collaboration between a volunteer and an incarcerated individual to create a portfolio of his or her best work.

The Prison Creative Arts Project's mission is to collaborate with these populations to strengthen our community through creative expression. We believe that everyone has the capacity to create art. Art is necessary for individual and societal growth, connection and survival. It should be accessible to everyone. The values that guide our process are respect, collaboration in which vulnerability, risk, and improvisation lead to discovery and resilience, persistence, patience, love and laughter. We are joined with others in the struggle for social justice, and we make possible spaces in and from which the voices and visions of the incarcerated can be expressed.

To learn more about PCAP, or to donate to our organization, please visit www.prisonarts.org.

CPSIA information can be obtained at www.ICGtesting.com
Printed in the USA
BVOW06s1950060316

439296BV00003B/3/P